Eagles over Darwin

AMERICAN AIRMEN DEFENDING NORTHERN AUSTRALIA IN 1942

Dr Tom Lewis

Avonmore Books

Eagles over Darwin

American Airmen defending Northern Australia in 1942
ISBN 978-0-6486659-8-4
Dr Tom Lewis

To Trevor and Pam

First published 2021 by Avonmore Books
Avonmore Books
PO Box 217
Kent Town
South Australia 5071
Australia

Phone: (61 8) 8431 9780
avonmorebooks.com.au

A catalogue record for this
book is available from the
National Library of Australia

Cover design & layout by Diane Bricknell

Cover artwork captions

Front: First Lieutenant Andrew Reynolds patrols over Darwin in his P-40E-1 Stardust / Oklahoma Kid.
(Michael Claringbould)

Back: A Takao Kokutai G4M1 Betty is attacked by a 49th PG P-40E over Darwin in April 1942.
(Michael Claringbould)

Contents

Acknowledgements 4

About the Author...5

Maps 6

Introduction 9

Chapter 1 – Buel, the First Hero 11

Chapter 2 – The 19th February Fight 17

Chapter 3 – The Reality of Aerial Combat 29

Chapter 4 – Arrival of the 49th Pursuit Group..................... 41

Chapter 5 – The Opponents: the P-40 versus the Zero and the Betty 59

Chapter 6 – The First Combats: March-May 1942 65

Chapter 7 – The Peak: June 1942 79

Chapter 8 – Final Months: July - September 1942 87

Chapter 9 – Postscript 97

Appendix 1 - The Oestreicher Incident 99

Appendix 2.. 104

Sources.. 105

Index of Names... 106

Acknowledgements

Special thanks, in alphabetical order, to:

- Bob Alford, Aviation Historian. Much of this book is based on preliminary research carried out by Bob over many years. Its use is much appreciated, although I am responsible for any errors.

- Kaylene Anderson, as always.

- Dr Peter Williams, military historian, for his insights and perceptive comments.

Some small sections of this book have appeared in the same author's earlier works *Carrier Attack Darwin 1942* (Avonmore Books, 2013) and *The Empire Strikes South* (Avonmore Books, 2017).

The author acknowledges the contribution of the Northern Territory Government, whose NT History Awards sponsored research in the USA.

Explanatory Notes

Allied codenames for Japanese aircraft are used as they are familiar to Western readers. However, this is not strictly historically correct as the terms did not emerge until around mid-1942. The exception is for the "Zero", named because it was the Type 0 naval fighter, and the name has become the most widely known. Its Allied codename was "Zeke".

The P-40s used over northern Australia in 1942 were all "E" models. These were properly known as Warhawks to the Americans, but in Australia the British name, the Kittyhawk, was more commonly used. Otherwise the fighters were simply referred to as "P-40s".

Dates for combat flights over Australia are given as the take-off times for the Japanese aircrews. A reading of the text will deduce the local time and date of a bombing raid.

About the Author

Dr Tom Lewis, OAM, is one of Australia's foremost military historians and the author of 18 books. A proud resident of Darwin where he teaches history to high school students, Tom is a former naval officer whose career included service in Iraq and Timor.

Other books by the author:

Atomic Salvation. How the A-Bomb Attacks Saved the Lives of 32 Million People. (Big Sky, 2020)

Darwin Bombed! A Young Person's Guide to the Japanese attacks of 19 February 1942 (Avonmore Books, 2020)

The Empire Strikes South (Avonmore Books, 2017)

Honour Denied – Teddy Sheean A Tasmanian Hero (Avonmore Books, 2016)

Carrier Attack Darwin 1942 (with Peter Ingman, Avonmore Books, 2013)

Lethality in Combat (Big Sky, 2012)

The Submarine Six (Avonmore Books, 2011)

Darwin's Submarine I-124 (Avonmore Books, 2010)

Zero Hour in Broome (with Peter Ingman, Avonmore Books, 2010)

Captain Hec Waller: A Memorial Book (co-author, 2008)

10 Shipwrecks of the Northern Territory (co-author, 2007)

Australian Naval Leaders (RAN College, 2006)

By Derwent Divided (Tall Stories, 2000)

A War at Home (Tall Stories, 1999 & multiple reprints)

Darwin Sayonara (Boolarong, 1991)

Sensuikan I-124 (Tall Stories, 1997)

Wrecks in Darwin Waters (Turton & Armstrong, 1992)

By March 1942 the Japanese had captured much of the Netherlands East Indies which lay directly north of Darwin. Key airbases were located at Ambon, Kendari and Koepang. Koepang was used as an advanced base by Japanese aircraft although its proximity to Darwin meant that it was within range of RAAF Hudson bombers. Largely for this reason the main Japanese airbase in the region was at Kendari. During the war Darwin was the only Allied base of any significance along the northern Australian coastline illustrated, and hence was an obvious target for the Japanese. During the final months of the 1942 air campaign Japanese forces were distracted by minor operations in the Tanimbar and Aru island groups.

The geography of Darwin was dominated by two large islands immediately north of the town. These were Bathurst and Melville Islands, collectively known as the Tiwi Islands. An RAAF observation post at Cape Fourcroy was situated right under the flightpath of incoming raids from Koepang, and was of vital importance in relaying raid warnings to Darwin. To the south of Darwin ran the Stuart Highway, and in early 1942 new airstrips were constructed at Livingstone (34-Mile), Hughes and Strauss (27-Mile). Batchelor airfield had been built just before the war, while Adelaide River had only a small civil airstrip. With Darwin itself exposed to raids, the 49th Fighter Group operated from Livingstone, Strauss and Batchelor with a maintenance facility at Adelaide River.

Glossary and Abbreviations

(Japanese terms are in italics)

AA	Anti-Aircraft
ABDA	American-British-Dutch-Australian
ABDACOM	American-British-Dutch-Australian Command
Chutai	Japanese aircraft formation normally comprised of nine aircraft.
CO	Commanding Officer
FCPO	Flying Chief Petty Officer (IJN)
FCS	Fighter Control Squadron
FG	Fighter Group
FS	Fighter Squadron
Flyer1c	Aviator First Class (IJN)
Flyer3c	Aviator Third Class (IJN)
FPO1c	Flying Petty Officer First Class (IJN)
FPO2c	Flying Petty Officer Second Class (IJN)
Hinomaru	The red disc on the Japanese flag representing the sun and also used as a roundel on Japanese aircraft.
HQ	Headquarters
IJN	Imperial Japanese Navy
Kodochosho	Battle Action Report (IJN)
Koku Sentai	Air Flotilla, the parent unit to multiple *Kokutai*.
Kokutai	An IJN air group, consisting of between three and six *chutai*.
Ku	Abbreviation of *kokutai*
LAAMG	Light Anti-Aircraft Machine Gun
NEI	Netherlands East Indies
NWA	North Western Area
PG	Pursuit Group
PMG	Postmaster-General's Department
POW	Prisoner of War
PS	Pursuit Squadron
RAAF	Royal Australian Air Force
RAF	Royal Air Force
RDF	Radio Direction Finding, i.e. radar
Shotai	A Japanese tactical formation typically of three aircraft.
US	United States
USAAC	United States Army Air Corps
USAAF	United States Army Air Force
USAFIA	United States Army Forces in Australia
USN	United States Navy
USS	United States Ship
WWII	World War Two

Introduction

For most of 1942 the entire air defence of northern Australia was operated by airmen from the United States.

That year was very nearly the end of Australia as a country. To those men the present nation owes a great debt.

For most of the year P-40 fighters of the United States Army Air Force bravely took on large formations of Imperial Japanese Navy Betty bombers and their Zero escorts. It was a life and death struggle for which the P-40 was ill-suited: it was never designed as an interceptor and had poor performance at high altitude. It was in these machines that inexperienced young American flyers pitted themselves against battle-hardened Japanese adversaries in their feared Zero fighters.

This is their story.

Young Americans had been fighting and dying in northern Australia since the early days of the Pacific War. The first to fall was Lieutenant Robert Buel. He died in his P-40 on 15 February 1942, in combat against a Japanese flying boat north of Darwin. A lonely sign marks his end, placed on Darwin's Esplanade near a gun from the destroyer *USS Peary*, sunk nearby by Japanese dive-bombers with the loss of 88 lives. It is about time something significant was named after Buel, as his death marked the beginning of a shared Australian-American wartime experience that underpins the strength of the present-day alliance between the two nations.

Major Floyd Pell died in combat four days later, leading his nine men against a massive air armada of 188 carrier aircraft intent on bombing Darwin. This they did with impunity, leaving Pell's P-40s (all except one), smoking wrecks scattered around the northern Australia capital. Pell had a wartime airfield named after him, but it is all but forgotten now except as a historical site on tourist maps. However, Pell's sacrifice was indicative of American intent in the early days of the war. They were here to fight, and if they could not win in those grim times, their faith in ultimate victory was unshakeable.

The days of February 1942 were dark indeed for Australians. Just four days before the bombing of Darwin the British fortress of Singapore had surrendered. Seen as impregnable, the fall of Singapore left Australian defence policy in tatters and the nation without a single modern fighter plane with which to defend its home territory. With Britain busy fighting for its own survival, Australia turned to America. It was the beginning of what is today known as "The Alliance" and it started in Darwin.

Dr Tom Lewis, OAM.
Darwin, Northern Territory
September 2020

The newly constructed Darwin RAAF base in late 1941, which after the start of the Pacific War became a key transit point for aircraft reinforcing Java and elsewhere. (Bob Alford)

CHAPTER 1

Buel, the First Hero

What led to a lone US airman taking on the Japanese far out to sea from Darwin in February 1942?

Following the raid on Pearl Harbor in December 1941, other US assets and bases across the Pacific had also been attacked. The largest US presence was in the Philippines, and by February the defending forces under General MacArthur continued to offer stout resistance. While the Japanese continued a regional offensive against the British in Singapore and the Dutch in the Netherlands East Indies (NEI), American planners hoped to reinforce the Philippines.

Before the war Darwin was a sleepy tropical outpost, but its location on the north coast of Australia lent it enormous strategic importance at this time. Any aerial reinforcements intended for Singapore, the NEI or the Philippines would transit via Darwin. Adding to its importance, Darwin possessed a huge deep-water harbour, refuelling facilities, a spacious Royal Australian Air Force (RAAF) base and related communications and logistics infrastructure. Indeed, there were no other comparable facilities to the east or west of Darwin over thousands of miles of northern Australian coastline.

Recognising the strategic importance of Darwin, in January 1942 the Japanese Navy tried to shut the port down using submarines to lay mines and conduct torpedo attacks. The plan failed, and one of the 80-man submarines, the *I-124*, was sunk by the corvette *HMAS Deloraine*. The submarine, intact and sealed to this day, still lies outside Darwin harbour. Following this loss, the Japanese kept a watchful eye on Darwin and were increasingly wary of the growing Allied activity there.

There were five main types of Allied aircraft present in the Darwin area at this time. These were Wirraways and Lockheed Hudsons of the RAAF, Curtiss P-40E fighters and Douglas A-24 dive-bombers of the United States Army Air Corps (USAAC) and PBY Catalina flying boats of the United States Navy (USN). The Wirraways were single-engine training aircraft used for short-range patrols around Darwin, while the Hudsons were militarised airliners used for coastal patrol and as light bombers. The PBY flying boats of the USN had withdrawn from the Philippines and flew long range maritime patrol missions.

It requires some explanation as to why USAAC P-40Es and A-24s were in Darwin. In fact, the RAAF had no modern fighters of its own in Australia at this time so the handful of P-40Es present was the sole means of air defence for the vast continent. After the attack on Pearl Harbor, a convoy carrying military reinforcements for the Philippines was instead redirected to Australia. Known as the *Pensacola Convoy* (named after the escorting cruiser, the USS *Pensacola*) these ships arrived in Brisbane in late December 1941. Among the cargo was 18 P-40Es and 52 A-24s, all packed in crates.

Subsequently these aircraft were assembled at Amberley, an RAAF base near Brisbane. This initially took time as trained mechanics and supplies of tools and spare parts were lacking. However, further P-40Es arrived by ship in January, and in these early weeks of 1942 enough fighters were hastily assembled and flight tested to equip three USAAC squadrons. A cadre of combat experienced pilots had been evacuated to Australia from the Philippines, and these men acted as leaders and instructors for trainee pilots arriving from the US.

Initially the plan was for these squadrons to fly via Darwin through the islands of the NEI to the Philippines. However, such was the speed of the Japanese advance that by the time the first of these units, the 17th Pursuit Squadron (Provisional), arrived in Darwin in mid-January the route through the NEI had been cut off. Instead this unit was directed to Java, which was the administrative and commercial centre of the NEI and where most of the defences were based. From Darwin the P-40Es flew a long over-water leg to the island of Timor, and then had one further refuelling stop at either Soemba or Bali before reaching Java.

Subsequently the route from Darwin to Java would cause much attrition to further flights of P-40Es (and some A-24s) using the route due to the tropical weather and the lack of maintenance facilities along the route. In addition, other P-40Es were caught during their refuelling stops on Timor and Bali and were destroyed by Imperial Japanese Navy (IJN) Zero fighters.

Overall, this was a time of much confusion and rapidly changing plans. A convoy had been

One of the first batch of P-40s assembled in Australia being made ready for flight testing at RAAF Amberley in early 1942. (Australian War Memorial)

assembled in Darwin with reinforcements for Timor, and there was an intention for 15 P-40Es to cover the movement of the ships as they departed Darwin. When the ships were approaching their destination the P-40Es would then make their own way to Timor in order to cover the unloading there. However, when the convoy was finally at sea, on 15 February, this had not eventuated and there were just two P-40Es at Darwin. These had been left behind due to mechanical faults when their own squadron had made the flight to Java some days previously. The fighters were made airworthy and began flying patrols over Darwin. Each of their USAAC pilots, Lieutenants Robert J Buel and Robert G Oestreicher, were to play notable roles in the days to come.

Fighter cover over the ships was of great importance. Ships – both naval and civilian – if exposed to enemy air attack were in great danger. As the Royal Navy had learned to great cost, ships were ill-equipped to fend off determined air attack. The sinking of the *Prince of Wales* and *Repulse* off the Malayan coast in December 1941 had underlined this. These had been armoured capital ships, with extensive AA armament, but both succumbed to air attack within a few hours, overwhelmed by sheer numbers of Japanese aircraft armed with bombs and torpedoes. So, air cover was essential for any naval operation. In Darwin in February 1942 this meant land-based fighters – the role to be played by plentiful Allied aircraft carriers in the Pacific was years to come.

A squadron of P-40Es of the 33rd Pursuit Squadron (Provisional) was making the long cross-continent flight from Amberley to Perth. The plan was to load them aboard the deck of the old carrier *USS Langley* at Fremantle and deliver them to Java. The fighters had reached Port Pirie in South Australia when they received orders to divert urgently to Darwin. Hence 15 P-40Es under the experienced Major Floyd Pell were on their way north to provide much-needed cover for the Timor convoy, although RAAF Darwin had not been notified, and the convoy had already departed. There were substantial difficulties with two countries trying to operate together, with different terminology – although they both at least spoke English – different equipment, routines, tactics and strategic understanding.

Meanwhile the convoy out of Darwin was steaming towards Timor, although trying to keep as south as possible during daylight. However, long-range four-engine H6K Mavis flying boats of the IJN Toko *Kokutai* were now active in the area. Operating from a newly captured base at Ambon, they now had the range to search the entire Timor Sea and would daringly approach the shipping channels just outside Darwin. Indeed, while the convoy was departing Darwin in the early hours, five H6Ks were taking off so to be over the search area in daylight. One aircraft was delayed by a couple of hours due to engine trouble. It was this aircraft that spotted the convoy at 1030 and commenced shadowing it. With the enemy aircraft staying out of gun range, there was nothing the convoy could do. Three hours later, the flying boat made a bombing run on the cruiser *USS Houston*, dropping a small 60-kilogram bomb that landed some distance away. The cruiser then radioed Darwin and requested fighter support.

Both Buel and Oestreicher were actively patrolling in their pair of P-40Es from the Darwin RAAF base on 15 February 1942 but for some reason only Buel could be contacted by radio. He

Buel's P-40E at Darwin RAAF base on the morning of his final mission over the Timor Convoy on 15 February. The port engine cowl has been removed for a spark plug change. (Bob Alford)

A Kawanishi H6K Mavis flying boat burns after being shot down. A similar scene played out in the Timor Sea on 15 February when Buel downed a Mavis. After making an emergency water landing its crew escaped in a rubber dinghy. The smoke plume from the burning Mavis was visible from ships in the convoy. (USAAF)

was directed to make an overwater flight to find the convoy some 130 miles away. Buel managed to find the convoy but could not initially sight any lurking flying boats. As an aid *Houston* fired in the direction of the Mavis. This worked and Buel sped over the convoy towards the enemy. What followed was a running duel of around 15 minutes as the flying boat slipped in and out of cloud cover. At one point the flying boat emerged over *Houston* and dropped further bombs, but without effect.

Finally, Buel got close enough to get some good strikes on the enemy with his 0.50-inch calibre machine guns. The flying boat caught fire. However, at the same time Buel's fighter also took hits from the 20mm cannon mounted in the tail of the Mavis. Even the sturdy P-40 could not absorb hits from such a heavy calibre weapon, and Buel was killed as his fighter plunged into the sea in flames. The flying boat too was crippled although the pilot managed to make a successful ditching, however the radio operator, FCPO Kinichi Furakawao, was wounded. He later died, although eventually the rest of the airmen reached Melville Island and were taken prisoner. None of those onboard the convoy knew these details. All they saw was a bright flash of light and then black smoke on the horizon. Buel was the first man to die in the defence of Darwin, and the very first casualty of aerial combat in the Australian theatre.

However, Buel's bravery had brought the convoy only a brief respite. It had now been spotted and was known to the Japanese. The destination was obvious, and the slow convoy could expect to be easily located within the confines of the Timor Sea the next day. Indeed, the Japanese were especially keen that these ships would not reach Timor, as at this very time they were busy organising their own Timor invasion forces. Ironically, by now ten USAAC P-40Es (of the 15 that departed Port Pirie) under Major Floyd Pell had arrived in Darwin. Late that afternoon Pell led some of these aircraft to cover the convoy, but there were no longer any enemy aircraft present.

By the following morning of 16 February, *Houston*'s convoy was crossing the Timor Sea, and was almost beyond the combat radius of the Darwin-based fighters. At dawn Pell himself led a wingman far out into the Timor Sea and located the convoy, now just 100 miles short of Timor. But the limited range of the P-40s meant they could not stay long, and they soon turned for home. Meanwhile Pell had directed two other fighters to search Bathurst and Melville Islands for traces of Buel, but without result.

At 1030, just as Pell was returning to Darwin, a message was received that enemy bombers had arrived over the convoy, but it was now far too late and too far away for Pell's P-40s to assist. In fact, it was an IJN combined force of 36 G3M Nell bombers of the 1st *Kokutai* and nine H6K Mavis flying boats of the Toko *Ku* that proceeded to attack the ships. Mainly due to a spirited defence put up by the cruiser USS *Houston* did the convoy emerge largely unscathed. However, most of the ships had suffered near misses and anti-aircraft ammunition was now depleted, leaving in question the ability to fend off any further air attacks. In addition, the ships would be at their most vulnerable while stationary and unloading off the Timorese coast.

Given these considerations, that afternoon the convoy was ordered to reverse course and return to Darwin. This proved to be a wise course of action as the IJN had launched an even stronger attacking force on 17 February which failed to find the ships. Subsequently on the morning of 18 February the convoy passed safely back into Darwin harbour. Arguably Buel's sacrifice was in vain, but a larger catastrophe had been avoided with the safe return of the convoy and its 1,500 Australian and American troops.

Lieutenant Robert Buel, USAAC, who was killed after he intercepted a Mavis flying boat on 15 February. (Bob Alford)

Lieutenant Robert J Buel

Robert J "Blackie" Buel was from Fresno County in California. Before military service he was a School of Forestry student at the University of California. He was awarded the Purple Heart after his death.

Buel's body and his P-40 fighter have never been found. In 1992 a memorial plaque to him was dedicated in Darwin by the American Legion, the equivalent of the Australian Returned and Services League. It can be seen next to the USS *Peary* memorial on the Darwin Esplanade. Buel is also commemorated at Tablets of the Missing at the Manila American Cemetery in the Philippines.

A USAAC P-40E fighter in Darwin in early 1942. (Bob Alford)

CHAPTER 2

The 19ᵗʰ February Fight

On the morning of Thursday 19 February, 188 IJN aircraft took off from four aircraft carriers for a surprise raid on Darwin. Together with a second raid that day comprised of land-based bombers, this would be the largest single Japanese air attack ever mounted in the wider South Pacific area during the war. Quite simply this was a raid of immense strength, and comparable to the Pearl Harbor attack which had crippled the USN Pacific Fleet. After passing over the Bathurst and Melville Islands to the north of Darwin, the huge formation crossed the mainland and then wheeled around to attack from the south. Kate high-level bombers would strike first, closely followed by Val dive-bombers. A large force of Zeros would protect these bombers and eliminate any Allied air opposition. Standing in their way were ten P-40E fighters of the USAAC's 33ʳᵈ Pursuit Squadron (Provisional).

Firstly, a little bit of background is needed to properly understand the disposition of the defending forces in Darwin at this time. After Lieutenant Robert J Buel's fighter had been brought down just four days earlier, the sole remaining P-40, piloted by Lieutenant Robert G Oestreicher, had been joined by ten new arrivals under Major Floyd Pell. Pell was an experienced airman: in fact, he was no stranger to Darwin having transited through the town multiple times in 1941 while travelling between Australia and the Philippines. However, aside from Oestreicher, none of his pilots had more than a few dozen hours on a P-40 – hardly the type ready to match the elite Japanese flyers. Pell did the best he could, and divided his pilots into two flights. Pell himself commanded A Flight, while Oestreicher (a new addition to Pell's squadron and not well known) commanded B Flight. Most significantly, there was no operational radar, no chain of ground observation stations and no effective fighter control organisation. Without some form of warning, the effectiveness of fighters was severely limited. Even by flying repetitive patrol circuits over Darwin, there was little chance of picking up and intercepting the enemy in favourable conditions prior to an attack taking place.

The P-40 tail numbers – as was the case with all available aircraft – were listed on a chalkboard in the RAAF Darwin operations room, which technically made them available to the RAAF station commander, should he see the need. Enemy reconnaissance aircraft had been active in the past few days and intelligence reports indicated enemy carriers present to the north.

However, for whatever reason, neither the RAAF Darwin station commander, Wing Commander Griffith, or the acting area commander, Group Captain Scherger, ordered Pell's P-40s to remain in defence of the vital base. To be fair this was a very confused time. The multinational American-British-Dutch-Australian (ABDA) command extended to Darwin but was primarily concerned now with the defence of Java. American P-40s had been transiting via Darwin to Timor and Bali and then to Java. However, these flights were risky, using primitive fields and with little in the way of weather warnings. And it was a bad time for weather: Darwin's sea port had seen limited operations for a week due to cyclonic conditions earlier in the month. Indeed, just after this weather had seemingly cleared, nine P-40s had left Darwin for Koepang in the afternoon of 9 February. After one aircraft returned to Darwin with engine trouble, the others had an uneventful flight over the Timor Sea, led by an LB-30 Liberator. But approaching the Timorese coast, they were confronted by a huge, dark, tropical rainstorm. All eight valuable planes were subsequently lost in crash landings or as their pilots bailed out. Fortunately, most of the men survived. This disastrous mission must have weighed heavily on the shoulders of Pell, who was tasked with making the same trip just over a week later.

Pell's orders were to base his squadron at Penfui, near Koepang, and cover the unloading of the Timor convoy. This mission was now clearly redundant, with the convoy returned, and the Japanese were just then taking possession of Bali. This blocked the ferry route to Java as well. Perhaps Pell was hoping the RAAF would order him to remain at Darwin? However, the command arrangements were muddled. Was RAAF Darwin to protect Australian territory or serve greater Allied strategy in throwing everything at the defence of Java? Darwin – and part of the north-west Australian coast – was nominally "ABDA territory". To iron out such complexities the Air Officer Commanding RAAF North West Area, Air Commodore Wilson, had recently departed for Java to confer with ABDA headquarters, and was absent.

To add to the uncertainty, the commander of the RAAF Darwin station, Wing Commander Griffith, was a relative newcomer, having only arrived on 1 February. Being new in the job in a newly formed command and with his boss absent, Griffith probably did not feel he had either authority or the confidence of his superiors to retain the P-40s. Presumably the acting area commander, Scherger, was equally unwilling to take such decisions until Wilson returned from Java with the authority. For this reason and even with the return of the Timor Convoy on 18 February, Pell still planned to make the risky over-water flight to Timor with his inexperienced squadron the following morning. Simply, his reasoning apparently was that he had not received any word from either the United States Army Forces in Australia command or ABDA headquarters cancelling the order.

Among the many large aircraft present in Darwin was a B-17 that was tasked with escorting the P-40s to Timor. That afternoon, a LB-30 Liberator arrived from Java carrying the US Army's General Hurley on a transport mission. This aircraft was assigned to carry mechanics and support crew for Pell. Another B-24A Liberator was due to arrive the next day and pick up Hurley. The Qantas Empire flying boat *Camilla* had arrived in Darwin harbour late that afternoon. Onboard was Air Vice Marshal Richard Williams, widely regarded as the founding father of the RAAF, who was returning from a two-year stint in the UK.

Those in Darwin were well aware of the exposed nature of the RAAF base, especially as the Japanese were occupying land bases to the north – such as Ambon – that potentially brought Darwin within the range of land-based bombers. The Darwin base included two large hangars that were impossible to camouflage. A third was being erected but Wilson had the foresight to change these plans and allocate the hangar to a rearward base he planned to create at Daly Waters. That location – 400 miles south – already was used by civil planes as a refuelling station and a small civil hangar existed there. It was too far to the south to be a potential target. For this reason,

Wilson sent No. 12 Squadron's Wirraways there as a way of protecting them from surprise attack. However, this move had been countermanded by the governing Air Board, and the machines were ordered returned to Darwin (although during the subsequent raid the majority were safely dispersed at Batchelor, a short distance south of Darwin). While operated under the designation as "general purpose" aircraft, the RAAF had recently ordered that the Wirraways not be used as fighters. This was after a disaster during the defence of Rabaul in late January when a force of Wirraways had been effectively shot out of the sky by carrier-based Zeros.

On 18 February while Pell's men were planning their move north the RAAF was planning the best route out of the enemy areas. Indeed, seven of the other American P-40 pilots, stranded on Timor after the disastrous 9 February ferry flight, were waiting for transport back to Darwin. It had been decided to evacuate both them and all of the RAAF men of the Penfui base, except for a small rear-guard. At dusk on 18 February six RAAF Hudsons landed at Penfui. They loaded up with the evacuees and departed at 0330 in the morning of 19 February.

Brian Winspear was a wireless operator/gunner on one of these Hudsons. He wrote in his own book later:

> Next day with two other repaired Hudsons, overloaded with 23 men each, we evacuated most of our ground staff from Koepang to Darwin, leaving at 3 am to dodge the Jap air raids. The aircraft was so heavy it took over half an hour to reach cruising height and five hours to reach Darwin. Shortly after we left the Penfui 'drome, it was attacked by a dozen Jap bombers and dive-bombers.

After five hours of flying, the Hudsons approached Darwin soon after dawn. Perhaps illustrating a lack of communication between the services, the army AA gunners were frustrated at the aircraft not using correct recognition and approach procedures and fired a short-fused warning shot. Little did they know it would be the first of thousands of rounds fired that day.

Unfortunately, the US pilots onboard the Hudsons had little opportunity to communicate with Pell's men. His P-40s were supposed to leave for Timor at dawn but had been delayed due to a coolant leak in Pell's aircraft. Eventually another pilot was bumped, and Pell took his aircraft. Hence ten, instead of eleven P-40s took off at 0915. After barely 20 minutes in the air, and barely out of sight of Darwin, Pell received a message from the American control officers at Darwin, relayed via the accompanying B-17. The cloud base over Koepang was reportedly only 600 feet. Pell's men would have to turn back, while the B-17 proceeded.

The Americans were now flying back to Darwin into the sun. Standard procedure was for one flight to remain aloft, to prevent the other from being "bounced" while landing. As Pell led his A Flight of five P-40s down to land at RAAF Darwin, B Flight, under Oestreicher, was detailed to fly a covering patrol above at 15,000 feet for two hours. They circled out to the west over the harbour entrance, with the pilots probably watching the landings of A Flight in between the regulation constant searching of the sky around them. As A Flight landed, B Flight was slowly climbing through 8,000 feet. The time was around 0950.

From his own report it seems that after seeing Zeros shortly before 1000 on 19 February,

Carrier-launched Zeros swoop onto a P-40E from Lieutenant Oestreicher's B Flight at the start of the huge raid against Darwin on 19 February 1942. (Michael Claringbould)

Oestreicher dived away from his B Flight formation yelling "Zeros, Zeros, Zeros" into his radio-microphone. Discharging his drop tank and diving away at high speed, he flew south, at low level and away from Darwin and was not seen again for over an hour (Oestreicher's subsequent claims in respect to the events of 19 February remain a subject of some controversy and are discussed in more detail in Appendix 1).

Meanwhile the other four pilots were set upon by Zeros, and in no position for an even fight. Lieutenant Bill Walker looked up to see nine Zeros peeling off from about 2,000 feet above, and diving on him and his element leader, Lieutenant Max Wiecks. The latter was preoccupied with getting his radio to function and was hunched over in his cockpit. The Japanese were in a near perfect position with surprise almost complete and attacking from above.

The subsequent combat is somewhat confused, but the outcomes are known. In a hopeless position, the American pilots bravely tried to turn into the Zeros and fight them. For the elite Japanese pilots, the dogfight was easy work. The P-40s could not outfly them, but they were well-built, with armour plate and self-sealing fuel tanks, unlike the Zeros. This saved the life of a couple of their pilots. After Wiecks' plane was hit, he found himself diving out to sea with dead controls. At 4,000 feet he struggled to bail out, just managing to do so in time. As his parachute opened fully, he heard his plane splash into the water below him, some ten miles off the coast.

Wiecks' wingman, Walker, had also tried to dogfight the attackers but almost immediately his P-40 took hits in the cockpit. Walker was wounded in the shoulder and was unable to detach his drop-tank. He dove for the airfield and landed, although at a high rate of speed with no flaps. However, Walker survived, unlike the other two pilots from B Flight, Jack Peres and Elton Perry. Little precise detail is known of their fates, although Peres was last seen being chased by a Zero. His aircraft was not found until September 1942, a good distance away from the airfield at Gunn Point. His remains were still in the wreck and were identified by his engraved wristwatch.

Perry had the unpleasant distinction of being the first airman killed over Australia, with his P-40 seen to plunge into the water off Casuarina Beach. The crash was observed by soldiers of the 2/14th Field Regiment at nearby Nightcliff, although the wreck was not found until years later by a Darwin City Council worker.

For ground troops, and others, the noise of the dogfights and the scene of diving P-40s was the first hint that a raid was in progress. At the RAAF base, Pell's A Flight had landed and by 1000 the five P-40s were being parked at the end of the runway. However, with frantic signalling from ground crews, and the excited chatter of their B Flight comrades on their radios, the five pilots realised a raid was in progress and scrambled to get airborne. Very quickly the five P-40s of A Flight were rapidly accelerating along the runway to join the fight.

At this time, with the Kate three-man attack bomber formations over the drop zone, many of those on the ground described them as appearing like perfectly arranged V's of tiny silver crosses. Pell and his pilots would have seen this too. They would have been intent on climbing to altitude as quickly as possible to catch the attackers. The last thing Pell would have anticipated was to find fighters at low altitude. But that is exactly what happened. Probably, even as they began their take-off roll, the P-40s were spotted by keen-eyed Zero pilots, probably of the *Akagi* fighter *chutai*, intending to strafe the airfield.

Pell was first into the air, followed by Lieutenant Charles Hughes. Hughes was shot down and killed almost immediately, crashing into the scrub just a mile or so from the end of the runway. In the first seconds Pell initially evaded the attention of the attackers by desperate flying at treetop level, but he was in a hopeless position with no altitude and little airspeed. Quickly Pell's aircraft was hit and fatally damaged. He bailed out of his P-40 at barely 100 feet. With no time for his parachute to open Pell was killed.

The other three P-40 pilots found themselves outnumbered and fighting independently against trios of Zeros. The next pilot to take off, Lieutenant Burt Rice, managed to reach 1,500 feet and manoeuvred against three enemy fighters before his plane was hit. He bailed out safely, albeit with an eye wound, ten miles east of the RAAF base. As Australian soldiers came to his aid, he was strafed from above.

Possibly as the nine *Akagi* Zeroes were taking on these three victims, it gave a narrow margin of opportunity to the last two pilots, who appear to have had some chance to get up speed and altitude. Lieutenant John Glover managed to reach 3,000 feet despite a wheel hitting an empty fuel drum at the end of the aerodrome as he took off. He was able to bring his guns to bear on at least one Zero, but he flew too low and crashed into trees on the edge of the field. Glover survived but was badly wounded.

The fifth P-40, flown by Lieutenant Robert McMahon, just missed colliding with the damaged plane from B Flight, flown by wounded Bill Walker, which was making a high-speed emergency landing. McMahon recalls that upon taking off:

> I picked up plenty of flying speed and established a minimum-altitude climb out so I could just barely clear the taller eucalypts on the far end of the field. In the process I automatically turned right to look over my shoulder and as I looked up, I saw six aircraft up there with radial engines and they looked like A-24s. Then I did a double-take and looked back and oh, oh! There were the big red meatballs.

McMahon was an easy target but did his best to make evasive manoeuvres. At one stage he exchanged fire with a Zero flying directly at him. The dogfighting at low altitude continued for some minutes until his P-40 took hits. His undercarriage became unlocked and fell down in the landing position, severely retarding his speed. Worse, his coolant system was leaking and he knew in a short time his engine would overheat and seize. He now found himself flying through the maelstrom of the dive-bombing and strafing attacks over the harbour. With his gear down, he somehow threaded his way through the crowded airspace, possibly taking friendly fire as he flew over the likes of the destroyer USS *Peary*. Knowing that the seaplane tender USS *William B Preston* and her Catalinas were at the end of the harbour, he figured the ship would provide some protection with her AA fire. But his aircraft was in trouble, and he soon bailed out.

The loss of McMahon meant there were no longer any P-40s in the air. Nine had been shot down or crash landed, while Oestriecher had fled to the south.

The raid, which had begun at 956, concluded quickly. The harbour and town were covered with smoke. Fires were raging in several places. Nine ships were sunk or sinking; 30 aircraft had been destroyed, and 235 people were either dead or dying, with hundreds more wounded. A large portion of those killed were Americans, with some 88 USN sailors lost on the destroyer USS *Peary* which sunk very quickly after taking direct hits from Val dive-bombers. Along with the four pilots killed, the USAAC also lost Staff Sergeant Hugh M McTavish, killed on the ground at the RAAF base near aircraft strafed by the Zeros.

The Kate high level bombers had left quickly once their ordnance was unloaded, flying off in formation. The Vals left one by one as they expended their single bomb. The Zeros, the attack dogs of the air armada, circled and strafed as opportunity arose, but kept ammunition for the flight back to the carriers. They too left gradually as their bomber charges flew off. By 1030 all of the attackers had gone, leaving the USAAC defenders shattered, as was the port and parts of the town. To make matters worse another air raid came in at 1145, of 54 land-based bombers without a fighter escort. They bombed with relative impunity and a deadly accuracy that left the RAAF base a smoking ruin.

The Japanese lost one aircraft, a Val dive-bomber, which crashed not far from the RAAF base. It was a victim of AA fire from the ground, of which there had been a great deal, especially from rifles and machine guns. Along with the army's 3.7-inch AA batteries, there had also been a great deal of return fire from the many naval ships in the harbour, and it is surprising that more

The wreck of Lieutenant Bill Walker's P-40E, who crash-landed at RAAF Darwin on 19 February. In the background is a water tower also used as an airfield control tower. (Bob Alford)

A soldier poses with the wreck of Lieutenant John Glover's P-40E, which crashed into trees shortly after taking off from the RAAF base and tangling with Zeros. (Bob Alford)

aircraft were not downed over Darwin. However, many of the attackers were damaged, and a few did not make it back to their home carriers. A Zero flying out of the harbour, suffered oil pressure loss after being hit by small arms fire. Its pilot elected to land on Melville Island to Darwin's north, where he was captured by a local Aboriginal man. Two more aircraft – a Val and a Zero – ditched on the way back to the carriers, with their aircrews efficiently collected by friendly ships.

With Darwin and its installations smashed, the Japanese went ahead with their Timor invasion operations largely unhindered. A short time later in March they captured Java, completing a lightning conquest of South East Asia, with the jewel in their crown being the capture of Singapore on 15 February. The news of the fall of Singapore and the then the bombing of Darwin came in quick succession to Australians, and both events deeply shocked the nation. The future looked extremely grim. Air defence of the entire continent of Australia largely fell to newly arrived trainee American pilots, backed up by a few surviving veterans of the Java and Philippine campaigns. Could they hold the line?

Lieutenant Jack R Peres

Lieutenant Jack R Peres was born in 1920, the son of Louise and the stepson of John Peres. Peres spent three years of college training to become an actor, and never married. He enlisted in the USAAC on 31 December 1940 at March Field, Riverside, California. Peres was posthumously awarded the Distinguished Service Cross by General MacArthur. Sections of his aircraft, including the engine, are on display at the Darwin Aviation Museum.

A display honouring Lieutenant Jack Peres at the Darwin Aviation Museum, featuring parts of his P-40. (Author)

Lieutenant Elton S Perry

Lieutenant Elton S Perry was born in Creighton, Maricopa, Arizona, in 1917, to Will and Jessie Perry. Perry was a skilled mechanic and repairman and did not marry. He enlisted as an Aviation Cadet in the USAAC on 31 December 1940. Perry was awarded the US Purple Heart Medal, in addition to receiving a posthumous award of the Distinguished Service Cross from General MacArthur. There was a monument to his death at Fort William McKinley in Manila, now the headquarters of the Philippine National Army.

Lieutenant Elton S Perry. (togetherweserved.com)

Lieutenant Charles Hughes

Lieutenant Charles Hughes was born in Massachusetts in 1910. He was a hotel clerk in Baltimore City, Maryland, before enlisting as a private in the USAAC at MacDill Field, Florida, on 24 June 1941. Charles Hughes was awarded the US Purple Heart Medal, in addition to receiving a posthumous award of the Distinguished Service Cross from General MacArthur. There was a monument to his death at Fort William McKinley in Manila, now the headquarters of the Philippine National Army.

Lieutenant Charles Hughes (Bob Alford)

Floyd J Pell as a cadet at West Point. (Bob Alford)

Major Floyd J Pell

Major Floyd Pell was born on 29 December 1913 in Ogden, Utah, to Wesley and Gertrude Pell. Aged 20, Pell enlisted at the United States Military Academy School, West Point, New York. He enlisted in the USAAC in 1937. Pell was engaged at the time of his death to Second Lieutenant Juanita Redmond of South Carolina. Redmond served as a nurse in the Philippines and was evacuated by air, seven days before the fall of Bataan in April 1942. She visited her fiancé's grave when she landed in Darwin. Major Pell was reburied in the United States Military Academy Cemetery, West Point, New York, on 30 September 1948. To honour Pell, Australia named a wartime airfield and a military camp after him. Pell Court in the suburb of Moulden, south of Darwin, is also named in his memory. He was posthumously awarded the Distinguished Service Cross by General MacArthur.

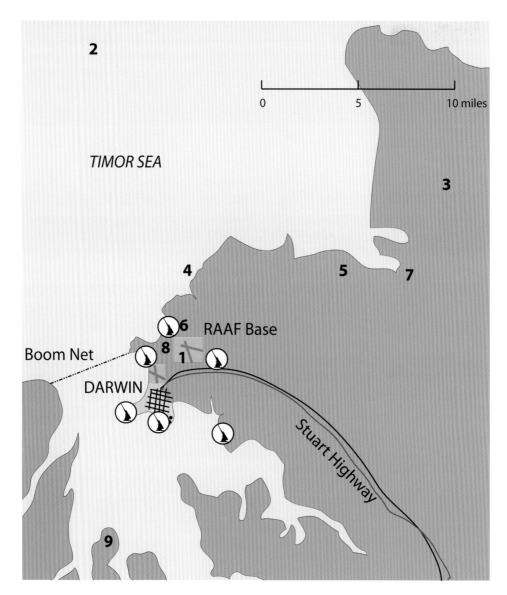

A map of the P-40 crash locations cross-referenced to the table opposite. The location of Australian army 3.7-inch AA batteries is also shown which all saw much action during the 19 February raid. The second airfield is Parap, the Darwin civil aerodrome which was located not far from the newly constructed RAAF base.

THE 19TH FEBRUARY FIGHT

Fate of the 33rd Pursuit Squadron pilots and P-40s, Darwin 19 February 1942.

B Flight	Fate	Map Ref	Notes
Lieutenant Robert Oestreicher	L	n/a	First to spot the enemy, Oestreicher dived away at high speed. He didn't return to the base until almost two hours later. A tyre burst on landing, but this was probably not due to combat damage. He flew to Daly Waters the next day in the same P-40.
Lieutenant William Walker	W	1	Wounded in shoulder, managed to land at RAAF base. Evacuated in hospital ship *Manunda* the next day. P-40 destroyed on the ground.
Lieutenant Max Wiecks	W	2	Bailed out over ocean. Eventually drifted ashore, spent night in mangroves and suffered exposure. Evacuated in *Manunda* the next day. Aircraft plunged into ocean north of East Point, around ten miles out according to the reports from the East Point rangefinder at the time. It has never been found.
Lieutenant Jack Peres	KIA	3	Shot down. Possibly had landed and taken off with A Flight. Wreck not located until September 1942, more than ten miles east of the base. Buried Adelaide River War Cemetery. Remains repatriated to US post-war and buried in home state of California.
Lieutenant Elton Perry	KIA	4	Shot down off Casuarina Beach. Body never recovered. Components of Perry's aircraft were recovered off Nungalinya, aka Old Man Rock in the 1960s, and other remnants including a gun bay panel were located along Casuarina Beach in 1995.
A Flight			
Major Floyd Pell	KIA	5	Attempted to bail out at low altitude but was killed. Body recovered and taken to Berrimah Hospital morgue. Buried in Darwin, then re-interred at Adelaide River War Cemetery in August 1942; post-war remains repatriated to the US and re-buried at West Point Military Cemetery. Pell's aircraft crashed at Camerons Beach near the current RAN remote outpost there; there are still remains *in situ*.
Lieutenant Charles Hughes	KIA	6	Shot down soon after take-off, crashing two miles from runway. Hughes' P-40 may have impacted on a site in Darwin's Trower Rd site, disintegrating completely and scattering its component parts over a large area. Remains not recoverable.
Lieutenant Burt Rice	W	7	Injured while bailing out ten miles east of RAAF base, in Shoal Bay area. Spent night in mangroves. Evacuated by *Manunda* the next day. His aircraft has not been recovered but there are reports of wreck parts found by a pig shooter in 1989, and Bob Alford found some P-40 components out in the Howard Swamp area.
Lieutenant John Glover	W	8	Flew into trees near RAAF base during dogfight. Survived crash with injuries. Evacuated on hospital ship *Manunda* the next day.
Lieutenant Robert McMahon	W	9	Bailed out over harbour mangroves with leg wound. Flown to hospital in Brisbane via Batchelor. Aircraft wreck never found. Is in mangrove country inland in the Milne Inlet area.
KIA – Killed In Action; W – Wounded; L = Landed unhurt.			

A Betty bomber which was the type responsible for most of the raids against the Darwin area in 1942. (Australian War Memorial)

An inside view of the cockpit of a Betty bomber. The crew spaces were cramped although the windows offered good visibility. (Timothy Hortman, National Air and Space Museum).

CHAPTER 3

The Reality of Aerial Combat

Northern Australia was assaulted by Japanese bombers from 19 February 1942 onwards. They were escorted by fighters. This chapter explains the reality of their strange world.

To fly in a World War II aircraft was to enter a world few other military men did. It was a strange surreal existence. An airman could leave a comfortable squadron base with hot meals, uninterrupted sleep and reasonable surroundings. Then once on a mission, he could be subject to the extremes of cold or heat, sometimes both. He could be cramped, uncomfortably crammed into a tiny cockpit or gun turret for hours on end. He could be bored, flying for hours often over territory familiar to him or featureless ocean before he reached enemy airspace. He was linked to the rest of the crew over an intercom, but idle chat was discouraged. Many airmen, if they were flying in the daytime, took a book to read before enemy territory was reached. If he was a flight engineer or a navigator however, he would be busy, monitoring the aircraft's vital systems if the former, or working out where they were and where they were hopefully going if the latter.

Once over enemy territory the situation changed. The enemy could be firing at him from fighters or with "flak" from anti-aircraft guns and his aircraft faced the risk of collision with one of the other bombers heading for the same target. He might shortly be fighting for his life; flinging the aircraft about the sky if a pilot; firing guns if he was a gunner and simply hanging on if neither. If he was wounded, he did not have the first-aid available even to an infantryman, for there were no medical personnel anywhere but back at his base. He could be experiencing all of this at night with its attendant mysteries and terrors.

If the airman survived he would be back at his squadron within hours, there to return to his comforts – although as the war deepened he was deployed further away from the trappings of civilisation. He might even be able to visit local hotels and towns or take leave. All of this was a pleasurable world denied to the infantry or to those in warships. Sometimes he faced the risk of his airfield being attacked. But if it wasn't for the terrors involved in "ops" it could sometimes be said to be a pleasant war. It was a very strange world for the airman.

Temperature and height

Next time you're flying in a modern airliner, experiment with the entertainment screen in front of you until you find the flight information. It will tell you amongst other things how high you're flying. If you're at an often-used cruising altitude of 36,000 feet – about 11,200 metres – you'll see it is about minus 50 degrees centigrade outside.

The aircraft at the beginning of the war were hardly heated; often just with some hot water radiators fitted with fans. The freezing temperatures could send airmen to sleep; highly dangerous for gunners who failed to see a fighter coming in from behind.

The dorsal gun blister position of a Betty bomber, showing a 7.7mm machine gun with a top-fitting circular magazine.

Some bombers were very much open to the elements. Max Sanders wrote of tail gunners:

> If Flip had wanted to toss [bricks and bottles] out of his part of the aircraft, he could because, like many rear gunners, he had removed the central part of perspex from the canopy of his rear turret to improve visibility … At the high operational altitudes, the open rear turret was not only a lonely place but also a very cold one – often with temperatures below -40C. Rear gunners were equipped with electrically heated boots and flying suits but, if these failed, frostbite was not uncommon.

In regard to the IJN Betty bomber, there were no conventional bomb bay doors. When loaded the bomb bay was left open to the elements with a deflector at the rear of the bay to reduce turbulence. At high altitude, even in the tropics, the cold was a serious factor and to combat it Betty crews had special electrically heated suits.

Pressurisation was also a factor. Air pressure drops as you ascend. This is why your ears "pop" as an aircraft in which you are flying climbs and comes back to earth: the air spaces contained within your skull are under pressure as they expand and contract. Aircraft in 1942 were non-pressurised, meaning that as the aircraft climbed, a person needed to breathe harder and deeper to obtain the same amount of oxygen for the brain and body. The heart and lungs have to work harder for the same result as obtained at ground level.

Both Allied and Japanese aircrews used oxygen when at high altitude, although supplies were limited and crews faced altitude sickness, or even death, without an adequate supply. A risk for fighters taking off in haste after an early mission was that the oxygen had not been replenished by ground crews.

Space to move?

The twin-engined Bettys which regularly pounded northern Australia were only a few metres wide – a long thin metal tube that was not designed for crew comfort. The machine was crammed with equipment for navigation and radio communication, together with defensive armament amid cramped positions for the aircrew. The gunner positions were sometimes in turrets which required small men to occupy convoluted crammed spaces often for hours at a time. Some were luckier in waist positions. Max Sanders recalled of his time in a Lancaster:

> It looked a huge plane on the outside, but when you got inside you could barely move about. I don't know how many times I bumped my head. The only place you could fully stretch out was in the emergency first aid bunk back behind Eddy's wireless station. It sure wasn't designed for comfort.

In fighters the pilot was wedged into the cockpit seat for the entire mission. He literally was strapped in with a harness that held him in tightly so his limbs would not flail about during high speed maneuvering. In front of him was a bank of instruments which he glanced across every few seconds, with the rest of his sweeping survey of the air outside, and of behind too, for this was where death might come in seconds.

Roles

The concept of specialised experts manning the aircraft was still in its infancy in 1939, but like all aspects of war technology, it changed fast. Hudson bomber crewman Brian Winspear, who flew out of Darwin, was a radio operator but also a gunner for his aircraft. Navigators (known as "Observers" in the RAAF in 1942 - a term dating from WWI) – were also part-timers with other roles, although as the need to navigate long distances, at night or over water became a reality this changed. By the advent of the long-range four engine bomber they were an assigned and recognisable expert member of the crew. Some forces used dedicated navigational aircraft as a variation or addition. The Japanese in particular used guide aircraft to lead the way – for example the March 1942 attack on Broome in Western Australia saw nine Zeros led by a two-man C5M Babs navigational guide aircraft.

Air gunners had added difficulty if they were in the nose or tail positions. Often their parachutes were not able to be taken with them, and so in the event of an emergency a gunner would have to crawl back up a tunnel and find their parachute, which was hooked onto part of the fuselage.

Bombardiers became a reality as accuracy in bombing became more pressing. If you wanted to hit an essential target you needed accuracy. Bombsights were invented – the Norden bombsight was the most famous of these – and there was a need for someone to guide the aircraft by looking through the bombsight directly at the ground from a bombardier position. Japanese bomber formations usually released their bombs on a signal from the lead aircraft and hence depended on a single bombardier. Over northern Australia this method often delivered surprising accuracy.

Mental stresses

It was psychologically difficult to become an aircrew member, given the stresses as outlined here, but the job of pilot was the most difficult. He had to be a master of a machine moving in

The author with Zero pilot Kaname Harada at his home in Nagano, Japan in 2015. Harada participated in the 19 February Darwin air raid. (Author)

three dimensions for a period usually of hours. He had to return the machine to the ground in one piece. Not only this, but he had to do it all at high speed, while often being shot at, or dealing with mechanical or electrical breakdowns or violent weather.

Kaname Harada was a Zero pilot who flew in the first Darwin air raid. He recalled his efforts at learning to fly:

> Mr Ejima who was my instructor was the person who worked his way up to the top from the ranks. He was my first venerable teacher and was one of the top instructors. In the exercise, he yelled out to me "no, no, idiot, what are you doing!" from the back of the plane during taking off and landing. I felt terrible. Even after all the efforts I had made to convince my parents to become a pilot, my path that I chose, and how hard I worked to enter the school, I thought maybe I am not meant to be a pilot after all if I get scolded by him like that all the time.

> That night I went to see Mr Ejima and said "Thank you for teaching me many things but I know what my limit is, and I don't think I am a gifted pilot. Please send me back to the team where I was. I am fine and I am ready to give up on this." And he said, "You misunderstand it. I scold students who have potential. The more I yell out, the more the person has potential. I try to maximise their abilities, not that I hate the person. I think you have a talent for this and I will keep yelling out to you. Please take this as my encouragement."

> I thought this could be the way to grow up. He is the person who I look up to giving me attention. I decided to keep going. Next day, he was as strict as yesterday. I was puzzled. He just convinced me to stay. I got confused if what he said yesterday was true... I was like, "Oh well... whatever" then I took my hands off the plane controls ... he then surprisingly said,

"Oh you are doing good, that's it! Keep going!" Before that, I was so nervous because he was telling me off. But all of a sudden, everything was changed from the moment I stopped pushing my plane around too much. Wow, this is it. I can fly!

Right from there, I realised that I was wrong…subconsciously I was arrogant towards my plane. I was always trying to manoeuver my plane. Each plane has its own character depending on who made it. Also each pilot has a different personality influencing the same aircraft. I was too immature to know this.

Personal eccentricities were forgiven to a fair degree in seemingly all air forces. RAAF member Ross Stagg, based at Strauss airstrip south of Darwin, recalls one of their pilots threatening on most days to shoot an inquisitive local bird that usually showed up around lunchtime, for its habit of "fouling the place." Zero pilot Saburo Sakai wore a belt made by two female friends for luck; they had stood on street corners in Japan and asked passing women for a stitch each, to make a "1000 stitch belt." Pilot Nishizawa Hiroyoshi, flying from Rabaul, was forgiven for a gruff exterior, because of his abilities:

[he] … cloaked himself in a cold, unfriendly reserve almost impossible to penetrate … he lived and breathed only to fly, and he flew for two things; the joy which comes with the ownership of that strange and wonderful world in the sky, and to fight.

Japanese pilots shot down were usually in despair at the disgrace they perceived they had brought upon themselves, by not fighting fiercely to the end. For example, pilot Yoshimitsu Maeda was brought down in Papua, but survived his Zero crash. He told his captors: "By becoming a POW he had automatically lost his nationality and would never be able to return to Japan and expressed the wish to be shot." Hajime Toyoshima, whose Zero crash-landed on Melville Island after the 19 February raid on Darwin, was captured and moved to the POW camp at Cowra, New South Wales. He kept his identity secret, and after helping to lead the failed Cowra Breakout of 1944, he killed himself rather than face recapture.

The basic rule of always keeping alert was essential – and was something that was unique to the world of air combat before radar. One of the most important parts of a pilot's anatomy, apart from his eyes, was his neck – it needed to be constantly turning to check his blind spots. Spitfire pilot Lysle Roberts, flying with No. 457 Squadron in the Northern Territory, recalled:

You never let the seat of your pants sit still. You're dancing around the whole time so if an enemy does get on your tail, he has difficulty in lining you up because you're moving. If you make yourself a moveable item the whole time, it's going to far more difficult for you to be shot down.

Saburo Sakai relates what happened when a pilot was not on the lookout. He and two wingmen stalked an American Airacobra in New Guinea:

The pilot seemed oblivious to everything; he maintained his course as we approached from behind and below …. I could see the pilot clearly and still could not understand his stupidity in not searching the sky around him. He was a big man, wearing a white cap. I studied him for several seconds, then dropped below his fighter. I aimed carefully before firing …

For all that, airmen affected a carefree camaraderie which was deceiving to outsiders. How could these young men not be stricken by grief when one of their fellow airmen failed to come back: simply disappearing, or being seen to go down in flames? But people came and went all the time on busy squadron bases, and sometimes the nature of a loss was not known. One's former comrade might be simply delayed for several days, and turn up unannounced, grinning in the back of a truck, having survived after their machine crash-landed or they successfully parachuted.

The flight

World War II aircraft contained a hazardous mix of high-octane fuel, electricity, ammunition and in the case of bombers their bomb load itself: explosives packed inside metal casings. The machine was driven by spinning propellers rotating at high speed at often less than a metre from the fuselage. Some aircraft were more prone to the risk of fire than others; the Betty for example was known by a reference to a cigarette lighter as the "One-Shot Lighter".

When an aircraft was working properly all went well, but there were a lot of combinations which could bring a machine undone. Weather was always a potential hazard, with wind, rain, storms and more to turn an operation awry. Flying weather varied, with cyclones and intense storms in tropical climes such as northern Australia. Navigation was done with much reference to the ground and having this hidden by cloud was an added difficulty.

The number of flights an aircrew member completed in a "tour" of operations varied with the force. In the Commonwealth it was set at 30 or 35 missions. The USAAF in the Pacific had a target of 30 but this was later revised to 40: this gave aircrew a 50% chance of being killed before reaching that target. The staff of the RAF's commander, Bomber Harris, made a ruling in August 1942 that 30 missions was the limit; then personnel were posted to six months at a training depot, before returning for a second tour of 20 missions. Sakai gives a varying number of deployments, but as Japan grew more desperate it seems to have expended its aircrew with less and less relief through instructional or test rotations, and leave became a rarity.

A completed bombing mission was one that took the bomb load to the target, or at least tried to. Missions undertaken by aircraft that took off and then turned back due to a failure of its systems or weather problems were not regarded as complete. This gave an impetus to crews to push on and complete their missions. Landing an aircraft with a full bomb load was also a considerable hazard.

Finding the way

WWII aircraft found it difficult to navigate, due to a combination of limitations of the technologies of the time and the actions of the enemy.

Flying low to navigate by using visual markers: rivers, roads, towns and so on, was fine except for the limitations of weather, which could force you low, towards the hazards of hills and mountains, or high above cloud, where you had to navigate by dead reckoning. This meant a combination of analysing that you had flown in *this* direction for *this* long at *this* speed, so therefore you had to be *here*. When flying in such conditions, allowances had to be made for the wind, and such reckoning could often be wrong.

In 1942 Japanese aircraft faced a long over-water leg from their forward base in Timor to reach the Darwin area. Usually their navigation was very good, aided by the generally fine weather of the 1942 dry season that lasted from approximately April to October. On occasion that bad weather was encountered over the Timor Sea the Japanese usually turned back.

In contrast during the Darwin wet season there is about six feet of rainfall, which arrives in short sharp torrential showers, sometimes so heavy that being out in such a storm is like standing under a fire hose. Needless to say, these were dangerous conditions for flying, as witnessed by the loss of eight P-40s to a weather system encountered as they approached Timor in February 1942. For this reason, the air fighting over Darwin was seasonal, and Japanese offensive operations were largely suspended during the 1942-43 wet season.

Basic fighter tactics

The fighters of WWII developed their tactics from those devised in the Great War, 20 years earlier. Surprise and aggression were crucial. Flying Officer RS Wortley explained the basic World War One German attacks in a letter to a friend:

> The tactics of the pilots seldom varied. They would climb to a height of about 10,000 feet whence they would swoop, hawklike, upon our machines as they passed below them, firing continuously as they dived ...The Fokkers hunted in pairs, sometimes, even three of them would fly together.

A book by the well-known American flier Eddie Rickenbacker is full of references to the standard tactical approach of shooting your enemy from behind before he saw you, preferably with the sun at your back to ensure any searching pilots were blind to the approaching killer:

> None of them had seen my approach. At fifty yards I pressed my triggers and played my bullets straight into the pilot's seat.

Thus the basic fighter attacking tactic became one of achieving surprise, and closing to within short and therefore effective range. The tactics of air combat were developed further in WWII. Erich Hartmann, with 353 confirmed victories, is one of the highest scoring "aces" of all time. His tactics included ensuring "the windscreen is filled with the enemy", and to always use the element of surprise. British ace Douglas Bader, famous for his artificial legs and refusal to quit combat, exhorted:

> He who has the sun creates surprise. He who has the height controls the battle. He who gets in close shoots them down.

Walter Krupinski, another high-scoring German WWII flier, also preferred to get close and to attack from behind the enemy:

> ... so he can't see you until it's too late.

Fighter pilot Major Gilbert O'Brien described a close range kill against a Japanese Zero:

> I was in range astern and closed on the Zeke to about fifty yards before firing. The first few shots burst on the right elevator. I fired until flames shot out from all parts of his plane. The enemy pilot appeared skilled and eager for combat but I don't believe he saw me.

Combat Claims

Some of the aerial combats over Darwin in 1942 were large scale affairs, with dozens of combatants on either side. Not surprisingly such combats were confusing with highly inaccurate claiming which was often the norm. For example, in an attack on Darwin on 25 April 1942 the defending American forces claimed 12 of the raiding aircraft shot down, while in reality the Japanese lost five. Not to be outdone in exaggeration the attacking Japanese claimed seven machines destroyed, while in fact no P-40s were lost, although three had been hit.

There were many reasons for such over claiming. Beginner pilots misidentified their targets, opened fire from too far away and often claimed victories that didn't exist. Multiple pilots might fire in the vicinity of a single doomed enemy aircraft, with each claiming it as their own victory. A smoking aircraft also was not necessarily a guarantee of a kill – it might be just damaged, and both the Zero and Betty were known to produce smoke under emergency power as they sought to escape.

With experience fighter tactics became better. Pilots were trained in how to best attack bombers. Pilots learnt to fire from behind at speed, preferably before the tail gunner got a sighting. Or they set upon bombers in packs, attacking from different directions, which divided the effectiveness of the defenders' gunners. Such improvements meant that with experience claiming accuracy also improved.

To an extent the over-claiming was encouraged at an official level, especially for American units in the South West Pacific Area. Commanders celebrated unit kill tallies and awards were liberally handed out, with such events being enthusiastically reported by the media. Overall, this was viewed as positive for the fighting morale of the aircrew involved.

Not to be outdone the Japanese press also repeated the extravagant claims. The *Japan Times and Advertiser* for 17 June 1942, claimed 20 "… modernly-equipped enemy planes" had been shot down during a Darwin raid, whilst the 27 August 1942 edition claimed a further 14 "…P-40 and P-39 type enemy fighter aircraft" had been downed in a raid on Hughes airfield. The actual losses were four and nil respectively.

An analysis of numbers such as the above shows that percentagewise it was not unusual for the actual kills as opposed to the reality being over-stated by factor of 100 to 500% or more. This was normal enough for World War II – see the author's *The Empire Strikes South*, which catalogues the reality of Japanese losses through the war over northern Australia. Such analysis as we have here shows us that routine disbelief is a better approach to aerial combat claims than mere acceptance.

Ground Defences

Death dealt by the enemy could come from a myriad of sources. At low altitude aircraft faced the threat of machine gun fire such as that which downed a Val dive-bomber over Darwin on 19 February 1942. This could be avoided by flying at medium altitudes, although some medium calibre weapons such as 40mm anti-aircraft guns were still a threat at such heights. Darwin was protected by 3.7-inch anti-aircraft guns which could reach high altitudes of up to 30,000 feet. These guns routinely engaged formations of Betty bombers during the 1942 air campaign.

When firing AA at such heights it took a considerable time, perhaps 20 seconds or more, for a shell to reach the target altitude. During such a time interval a bomber flying at 250 miles per hour would cover more than a mile in horizontal flight, so the AA battery had to aim considerably in front of the target, along the predicted flightpath. A moving barrage was then put up with the shells fused to explode at the estimated height of the target. Direct hits on aircraft were exceedingly rare, and instead it was hoped that shrapnel from the exploding shells would damage the enemy bombers. As bombers had to fly straight and level during their bombing run they were vulnerable to well-aimed AA fire, and over Darwin the 3.7-inch batteries proved accurate.

After dropping their bombs, the Bettys usually entered a shallow dive to lose altitude and gain speed, a tactic which greatly complicated the aiming process for the AA guns. Another factor in AA fire was the presence of friendly fighters, and over Darwin close liaison between the Australian AA guns and the ground controllers of the American fighters was soon established. The AA guns would generally hold fire when the fighters were intercepting the bombers.

By the time of the February 1942 raid, the Darwin area already had a reasonably well-established system of AA defences, which comprised the 2nd and 14th Anti-Aircraft Batteries as detailed:

14th Anti-Aircraft Battery
No. 1 Section: 2 x 3" guns, Elliot Point
No. 2 Section: 4 x 3.7" guns, Darwin Oval
No. 3 Section: 4 x 3.7" guns, Fannie Bay
No. 4 Section: 4 x 3.7" guns, McMillans
LAAMG Troop, 8 x Lewis MGs, Oil Tanks

2nd Anti-Aircraft Battery
"Berrima Section": 4 x 3.7" guns, Berrimah
LAAMG Troop: 8 x Lewis MGs, Berrimah
"Quarantine Section": 4 x 3.7" guns (under construction); crews at Berrimah as spares
No. 1 Section: 4 x 3" guns, Batchelor

These defences were augmented considerably during the course of 1942. Over time the levels of cooperation and understanding between various ground-based defences grew, including that of observation posts, radar, AA, searchlight and fighter control units. Such cooperation between these forces meant better effectiveness at combating bombers. Effective AA fire also forced the incoming bombers to fly higher which decreased bombing accuracy. On occasion the exploding AA shells aided fighter pilots in sighting enemy formations, something that was often difficult at long range in Darwin's bright tropical sunshine.

In theory, having a fighter aircraft available to shoot down an oncoming bomber was a better solution than AA fire. In practice, it wasn't that simple. The fighter had to be at the right height, in the right place, and intercepting at the right time. The whole scenario was also a very fluid one, as aircraft moved both horizontally and vertically, and at high speed. Fighters in particular are limited by fuel, and P-40s would burn a great deal of it while trying to climb to altitude, especially in an interception scenario.

Indeed, over Darwin it was impossible for P-40s to reach the altitude of the incoming Japanese formations after they had been spotted visually from Darwin. What was needed was a system of advance warning and in the Darwin environment this meant radar. By the start of 1942 the lessons of the Battle of Britain in 1940 had been well disseminated within both the RAAF and the USAAC. That experience demonstrated the effectiveness of radar warning combined with a fighter control organisation in combating enemy bomber incursions. Fighter control tracked the bombers using radar stations and then used radio communications to direct friendly fighters to make an interception.

In Darwin radar played a critical role in detecting enemy formations early enough to enable the fighters to take-off and climb to the altitude of the enemy which typically took at least 20-30 minutes. There was no functioning radar in Darwin at the time of the 19 February raid, but by the following month the first set was operational. The cover was continually improved over

Lookouts belonging to an AA battery watch skywards from an observation post on a rock formation near Batchelor. Many such posts combined with radar stations to track incoming formations and report updates on their movements. (Bob Alford)

subsequent months and it enabled interception of most of the incoming raids. The information from the radar stations was backed up by that from visual observation posts which could often give an accurate description of the raiding force.

The Darwin Environment

Downed pilots faced a hostile environment around Darwin. Landing in such areas was the stuff of Boys' Own adventure stories. Crocodiles feature in quantity in areas near the sea, as well as in river areas, where the fresh-water and less dangerous Johnstone's crocodile can be also found. The saltwater versions can grow up to six metres in length and attack humans.

In addition to such hazards, Northern Territory waters feature a deadly "box" jellyfish. With tentacles that reach up to three metres in length, they are almost invisible in water. Their sting can kill an adult in less than five minutes if they strike across the heart or face.

If aircrew made it through the sea, mudflats, and mangroves – the habitual home of both crocodiles and jellyfish – the more mundane fauna of the Territory awaited. There are several species of deadly snake and spider in northern Australia, as well as feral buffalo, and the native dog, the dingo.

With such hazards, as well as the tropical heat and humidity, a pilot bailing out of a stricken aircraft was almost literally out of the frying pan into the fire.

Major General Paul B Wurtsmith in a post war photo. Wurtsmith was appointed as commander of the 49th Pursuit Group in late 1941 and rapidly transformed it into a first-class fighting unit.

CHAPTER 4

Arrival of the 49th Pursuit Group

The days following the 19 February raid were tense. The battered defenders of Darwin were expecting further air raids, or even an amphibious attack, but it was not to be. Instead isolated Broome in Western Australia was struck. Nine Zero fighters guided by a Babs navigation aircraft hit the small settlement on 3 March. The raid destroyed many large aircraft and flying boats which were using Broome as an evacuation route from Java. Some 86 people died, making the Broome attack the second most deadly raid on Australia.

The following day a similar sized raid of nine Zeros, led by a single Babs, departed Timor bound for Darwin.

Upon arrival the Zeros strafed the RAAF base, destroying a RAAF Hudson and damaging the control tower along with a number of buildings. Railway gangers working nearby were also strafed by two Zeros. Landing back at Koepang the pilots claimed the Hudson and four aircraft destroyed on the ground. Three Japanese aircraft suffered minor damage from ground fire. This was the last raid in which the Japanese were to fly unchallenged by Allied fighters over Darwin.

On 17 March Captain James Selman, the commanding officer of the 9th Pursuit Squadron, 49th Pursuit Group, led thirteen P-40s into Darwin. He had already lost 12 of his original 25 aircraft due to mechanical problems and accidents. The latest had been on arrival at Daly Waters, just a few hundred miles south of Darwin, where Second Lieutenant Albert H Spehr crashed and was killed. It was caused by the normal but sometimes dangerous exuberance of fighter pilots. Ron Buckingham, a member of No. 13 Squadron, RAAF recalled:

> He tried a roll with his drop tank half full … his logbook recorded only nine hours on the P-40 type.

Aware that they had landed in the main target area for the Japanese, Captain Selman moved his aircraft to Batchelor the next day, about 50 miles south of Darwin, where they were welcomed enthusiastically. However, there were doubts, as noted in a contemporary report by Captain John E Doherty, USAAC:

> The presence of P-40s at nearby Batchelor Field has helped the morale at Darwin considerably … [but] it is likely, in my opinion, that the P-40s will not be of much value because: a) There is practically no warning system and the DF [a reference to Radio Direction Finding, i.e. radar] has never been in working order; and b) It seems that a fairly large percentage of the pursuit pilots at this field have had relatively little experience in P-40s or in combat tactics.

Born in conflict

The 49th Pursuit Group was formed in a world in crisis. Back when the USA was not yet involved in World War Two, on 17 October 1940 a War Department directive had ordered the raising of the new unit as part of a rapid expansion of the Army Air Corps. On 20 November the Group, comprising just a Headquarters and Headquarters Squadron was formed. Two months later the Group and its three squadrons, the 7th, 8th and 9th Pursuit Squadrons were activated at Selfridge Field, Michigan, under Major Glen Davasher. However, his tenure was brief. After being hospitalised, Davasher was replaced by Major John F Egan on 17 February 1941.

Initial manning of the new unit comprised officers and enlisted men from the 1st Pursuit Group, while the squadrons were manned by a token staff of officers. The command of the Headquarters and Headquarters Squadron was assigned to First Lieutenant Robert D Van Auken. Enlisted men, including mechanics, commenced arriving from mid-February, while the officer ranks swelled in answer to President Roosevelt's call for the return of reservists to active service.

A number of obsolescent Seversky P-35 aircraft were allocated to the new unit from the 1st Pursuit Group. These allowed the pilots to commence training flights around the local area. By March 1941, the 49th Pursuit Group had developed into a reasonably efficiently organised and administered unit, despite being under-manned and poorly equipped. The Air Corps however considered it had developed enough to warrant deployment. On 16 May 1941 the Group was ordered to Morrison Field, at West Palm Beach in Florida.

Three days later a 75-vehicle convoy left Selfridge Field. With only brief stops for fuel and rations, it arrived at Jacksonville, Florida four days later. The fifth day was spent on maintenance before entering Morrison Field on 25 May. The 49th PG then began attaching personnel to the various technical training schools, while a number of aircraft were allocated for pilot training. Each of the squadrons was provided with five aircraft: one Stearman PT-17, a Ryan PT-13, three Seversky P-35s and a Curtiss P-40B. The three P-35s were considered obsolete. As an 8th Pursuit Squadron armament mechanic, Dan Regan, commented:

It wasn't much but it was better than nothing.

Developments in Radio Direction Finding saw the 49th PG send ten enlisted men to Drew Field in Florida for training with the new technology, on 19 August 1941. There they studied methods of interceptor control, which was to play a vital role during the Group's time in Darwin.

During August and September 1941, the 49th PG participated in large war games, held in Louisiana. While gaining valuable experience, the Group also suffered its first loss in the air on 20 September. Second Lieutenant Carlyle Overud was killed when his aircraft crashed and burnt near Jackson, Georgia.

By late 1941 the possibility of conflict with Japan increased dramatically in response to an economic blockade imposed by America, Britain, the Netherlands and Australia. The 49th PG was caught up in the increased activity of a rapid expansion of the USAAC. More personnel were assigned, including Second Lieutenant Howard D Cory, whose time with the Group was short lived. He died when his P-40 aircraft flew into a fog-shrouded hill near St Louis on 18 December.

On 28 November 1941, newly promoted Major Paul B Wurtsmith was posted into the 49th PG as its commanding officer. Commencing Air Corps flying training in 1927, Wurtsmith had worked as an instructor, been a squadron commander and had served in the Philippines. He had 4,800 hours flying time and had flown virtually every type of aircraft in the USAAC inventory. His Operations Officer Major Donald Hutchinson was also experienced, with 2,600 hours to his name.

Wurtsmith immediately set about preparing the 49th PG for action. Inexperienced, poorly equipped and with no combat experience, the organisation had a huge learning curve ahead of it. However, Wurtsmith would prove to be an outstanding commanding officer and leader who would rapidly transform the young unit.

After the devastating attack by six IJN fleet carriers against Pearl Harbor on 7 December 1941 (American time), Japanese attacks on Malaya and the Philippines followed. The result was Japan and the US being dragged into a world conflict already involving Britain and Australia. Before long American involvement in Australia's future was foreshadowed in a report by Major-General Dwight D Eisenhower, who reported on 14 December to the United States Army Chief of Staff, General George C Marshall, that:

> ...our base must be Australia, and we must start at once to expand it and secure our communications to it. In the last we dare not fail.

The 49th on the move

With America entering World War Two, the 49th PG was placed on an immediate war footing, with the emphasis on preparing for combat. Training increased, while rumours were rife over the Group's future role. Many believed that its relative youth would see the Group assigned to guarding the US east coast; others believed they were destined for South America or the Panama Canal Zone.

On 19 December a fifth squadron was formed when the Interceptor Control Squadron was activated, with its modest initial function pertaining to the maintenance of a group operations plotting board. Command of the unit was assigned to First Lieutenant Van Auken, who however was also assigned to command the 8th Pursuit Squadron on 27 December. He retained command of the new unit as a secondary duty.

A further 37 pilots arrived on 21 December, further boosting the Group's manning. Three days later four officers and 28 enlisted men arrived to set up the Group's medical service under Captain Rosser B Ramsay.

Major Donald Hutchinson was appointed Group Operations Officer on 24 December while a further lot of pilots arrived. One of them was Second Lieutenant Clyde H Barnett Jr, who typified those early arrivals. Born at West Palm Beach in Florida, he had graduated with a bachelor's degree in electrical engineering from the University of Florida in 1940. Gaining his private pilot's licence, Barnett enlisted as a flying cadet with the USAAC on 26 April 1941. Following primary training, he completed his basic flying training and graduated as a Second

Lieutenant on 12 December 1941. That same day he married Janet Williams of Orlando.

Barnett recalled that following celebrations of both graduating and marriage, he typically:

>...filled out a lot of papers and waited for orders. At first I was assigned to Panama but that was cancelled. We had to wait around ... nearly two weeks waiting for orders. On 21 December [we] got orders to report without delay to Morrison Field ... I reported to the 49th Pursuit Group ... and was assigned to the 8th Pursuit Squadron.

The new arrivals were able to get some flying in, and Barnett logged one hour in a PT-17 and two hours in a BT-13 – both trainers. Rumours on the 49th PG's future persisted, until on Christmas Day orders to prepare to move at 72 hours' notice were received.

Over the following days personnel packed equipment and stores, while some had time to take care of their personal affairs and spend time with families. On New Year's Eve, Clyde and Janet Barnett:

>... went out to the Palm Tavern where they had a piss poor show ... we left and went over to the beach and watched the moon come up. It was beautiful.

Confined to base overnight on 2 January 1942, personnel departed by train the following morning. Morale was high despite the cramped conditions and men passed the time by reading, playing cards or board games, or watching the passing countryside. Five days later they arrived in San Francisco. The officers were taken to the Whitcomb Hotel while the enlisted men were accommodated at a huge covered arena, the California State Livestock Pavilion, known as the "Cow Palace".

One who recalled the Cow Palace was Private Ralph L Boyce. Little thought had apparently been given regarding any trade or skills these men possessed. After enlisting on 3 October 1941 and for almost a month after Pearl Harbor, he had:

>... languished [at] Jefferson Barracks, Missouri ... [until] in the early part of January ... [we] were suddenly shipped to 'Frisco ... a couple of days at Angel Island in 'Frisco Bay and a few more days ... in a huge livestock pavilion known as the Cow Palace.

Few assigned men, like Boyce, had any prior experience in the military, let alone in a technical environment such as the Air Corps.

Personnel were issued clothing and personal equipment. At dusk on January 11, personnel boarded the Matson Lines ship *Mariposa*. Boarding went on until late that night. As each man lugged his personal gear up the gangway, he was handed a pith helmet and a gas mask. In the late afternoon of 12 January 1942 the *Mariposa*, along with the President Lines ships *President Coolidge* and *President Monroe* sailed from San Francisco, escorted by two destroyers and the light cruiser *USS Phoenix*.

Fifty-one Curtiss P-40 fighters, 19 of them on *Mariposa*, were part of the cargo. On board the *Coolidge* were also the personnel of the 808th Engineer Battalion (Aviation) who were destined to construct airstrips in the Northern Territory.

The voyage across the Pacific aboard the *Mariposa* convoy had been seen by some of the airmen as nothing but boredom. It was, according to Clyde Barnett, a cycle of:

> … breakfast, [then] loaf, sleep, read, walk the deck, play shuffleboard, play cards, and every afternoon a meeting with Van Auken. Nearly every day somebody gave a talk on something they didn't know much about …

Ralph Boyce however saw the voyage as a mix of adventure tinged with mild excitement. He wrote that:

> … on Monday 12 of Jan we sailed under the Golden Gate …Then followed three whole weeks of ocean travel … Gorgeous sunsets, the breath taking blue that is the Pacific, the clean salty smell of the air; all this helped to make up for the cramped quarters, the nightly blackout, the everlasting tension from not knowing from where or when [an] attack might come.

While rumours regarding the 49th PG's destination circulated, Australia was confirmed when the *Mariposa*'s captain advised Wurtsmith that their destination was Melbourne. Two Royal Australian Navy cruisers joined the convoy on 29 January. The next morning, Sunday 1 February, Clyde Barnett recalled:

> …we woke up to find ourselves steaming past some big rocky headlands. The crew told us it was Wilson's Promentory (sic) and we were coming into Melbourne … the next morning we pulled into the dock.

However, Ralph Boyce recalled that no crowds lined the docks and the wharves were practically deserted. Disembarking, the men were transported by tram to a camp at Royal Park, where their initial lack of welcome was reversed:

> When we boarded that dinky little train (sic) … we got some indication of the warmth with which the people of Australia welcomed us. Waving wildly, some even with US flags, and cheering themselves hoarse … they let us know we could make ourselves at home in Australia.

On arrival at Royal Park the men marched in to the tune of *The Star Spangled Banner* played by an Australian band, and after a short welcoming speech the American flag was raised for the first time during the war in Melbourne.

Leaving the Interceptor Control Squadron behind to assist in unloading the convoy, the remaining 49th PG personnel were transported to Spencer Street railway station where they boarded a train. They travelled to the township of Bacchus Marsh some 35 miles west of Melbourne, where they then marched five miles to a barren Australian camp, named Camp Darley. Over the next two weeks the men were issued daily passes to Melbourne, got to know the locals, hunted rabbits to supplement the poor rations, and one man, Second Lieutenant George "Pinky" Davis, managed to get married.

Little did the USAAC men know however, that they were destined not to fight for the US war effort just yet. First came the job of comforting the locals. The Combined Chiefs of Staff in Washington had advised the Supreme Commander of ABDACOM, General Sir Archibald Wavell, that in order to meet the immediate need for Australia's northern defences they were turning over one USAAC pursuit group to the Australians to be under the command of the RAAF:

> It is to be the next Group to be completed and prepared for operations from the US personnel, and equipment now in, or arriving [in] Australia ... As Commanding General of the US Base facilities and communications for ABDA in Australia you will have the additional duty of supplying and supporting the US Pursuit Group detached for service with the Australians.

The stay at Bacchus Marsh came to an end on 14 February when the 9th Pursuit Squadron departed Camp Darley to board a special troop train, reaching Sydney the next day. Following a short break, they continued on to Newcastle some 100 miles north and from there to the nearby RAAF Williamtown air base.

The same day the Interceptor Control Squadron left Royal Park, following the remainder of the Group, which had departed Bacchus Marsh that morning. Travelling by train, they reached Queenbeyan on Canberra's outskirts on 18 February. From there the 8th Pursuit Squadron was transported to Fairbairn RAAF station. The main group, comprising the Headquarters and Headquarters Squadron, the 7th Pursuit Squadron and the 43rd Air Materiel Squadron, travelled on to Sydney, and along with the Interceptor Control Squadron were transported to the Bankstown No. 2 aerodrome, dubbed "Yankstown".

Fairbairn's Operations Record Book reported that:

> Lieutenant R D VAN AUKEN arrived by rail, 163 personnel, 45 officers, 118 men. Pilot Officer LOFT and Pilot Officer CHANNON reported for duty with 8th Pursuit Squadron.

The RAAF personnel, joined by Flying Officer Arthur Gilbert, were to undertake liaison duties and assist with flying training on P-40s in expectation of the RAAF receiving those it had on order. Other RAAF personnel were assigned to the 7th and 9th Pursuit Squadrons. Flight Lieutenant BM Cox was assigned to Station Headquarters at Fairbairn to liaise with the 8th PS while Flying Officers JW Norton and AD Tucker went to the 7th PS.

On 17 February, 90 personnel including four officers were sent to the Aircraft Erection Depot at RAAF Amberley west of Brisbane, to assist in the assembly and testing of the Group's P-40s. Other depots at Archerfield near Brisbane, along with Geelong and Laverton in Victoria, oversaw the assembly of the P-40s from the *Mariposa* convoy. From those locations the aircraft were flown to their units by USAAC and RAAF ferry pilots.

At Fairbairn, Bankstown and Williamtown, the 49th PG was to train for combat, but not without difficulties. The new P-40s had considerable torque in their liquid-cooled Allison V-1710 engine. The airmen had received very little preparation for flying such a relatively powerful aircraft in their very limited flight times.

Training Operations

On 19 February Wurtsmith received some good and bad news almost simultaneously. He was advised of his promotion to Lieutenant Colonel, effective from 5 December 1941, but also the

In the first weeks of operations in Australia the 49th PG experienced a high accident rate. This P-40 is being transported to the 43rd Air Material Squadron at Adelaide River for repairs after a landing accident at Darwin on 24 March.

information that the Japanese had mounted a devastating attack by carrier-borne aircraft on Darwin that morning.

For the pilots and ground crews hopeful of training on the new P-40s, they were initially disappointed. Barnett wrote:

> All the planes they had … were "Wirraways" (modified AT-6's) (sic) [we] called … Whirraways or Whizzaways. We were assigned four of them so we could get in some flying time until we got our P-40's. The Wirraways were not as good as our AT-6.

However, the first P-40s were not far away, as pilots were sent to the Geelong depot and RAAF Laverton to ferry P-40s to their bases. The 9th PS received its first two on 22 February and four days later the 7th PS also had some. Other pilots with very little or no experience on the type were sent by train to Brisbane to do a conversion course on P-40s run by experienced instructors, prior to ferrying more P-40s back to their squadrons.

On 23 February First Lieutenants Bob Morrissey, Robert Van Auken and James Selman were each promoted to captain and given command of the 7th, 8th and 9th Pursuit Squadrons respectively. At this time Corporal Kates of the Interceptor Control Squadron was sent ahead to Darwin and became the first 49th PG member to reach the combat area.

As the squadrons received their P-40s, pilots were rostered to ensure they were in the air as often as possible, though some only managed one hour and fifteen minutes flying each day. However long periods of inactivity had taken their toll. Since leaving Morrison Field several weeks earlier, most of the pilots had flown only briefly in the Wirraways assigned by the RAAF. Only five pilots had more than 600 hours on fighter aircraft. Wurtsmith and Hutchinson were two of them, while nine others had some 15 hours. The remaining 89 pilots had no hours at all on fighters.

It was a situation where many accidents were waiting to happen. The dubious honour of having the first accident went to Second Lieutenant Frederick O'Riley of the 7th PS. On 23 February he made a forced landing two miles west of Bankstown, ripping up 15 metres of fencing before crashing through the wall of a house and coming to rest in the kitchen. O'Riley suffered only a gashed lip and wounded pride. The same day saw Second Lieutenant John D Livingstone walk away from his P-40 after the undercarriage collapsed on landing at Williamtown.

Minor accidents were reasonably common, although fortunately few resulted in serious injury to the pilots. For the mechanics who put so much effort into maintaining the aircraft it was heartbreaking though, as all too often their efforts to provide an efficient and safe aircraft disappeared in a cloud of dust and a tangle of twisted metal.

By mid-March, the Group had suffered 22 training accidents with seven aircraft written off and three fatalities. Sergeant Norm Wilford recalled:

> … the aircraft lost at Williamstown (sic). Seven on one afternoon. The P-40 had a very narrow … main landing gear and the new pilots were not experienced … It was also a tail dragger and top heavy with that Allison engine. I am glad I did not have to fly it but the wing made good shade …

Ralph Boyce wrote how he had:

> …sweated out accidents and near accidents in and around the drome, [and] have seen several ships demolished & one pilot seriously injured. I even reached the point where I thought I was immune to any emotion over the loss of a plane or pilot. I was wrong.

Boyce was commenting on the death of a comrade. He had become friendly with Second Lieutenant Frank L Stiertz while working with him in the operations department, after Stiertz had reportedly been grounded for flying under the Sydney Harbour Bridge. On 14 March, Boyce arrived back at base and was informed that Stiertz had:

> … come in for a landing, started to ground loop, and in an attempt to save the plane had tried to take off again [but] … couldn't get the altitude … Desperately he gave it rudder … only to crash smack into the corner of the hangar. The ship burst into flames almost immediately. The crash crew got the flames out but it was hours before his body could be gotten (sic) out of the twisted wreckage.

Two others who died were Second Lieutenants John J Musial and Neal T "Sonny" Takala. They had been part of a four aircraft gunnery training sortie on 19 March. Flying with Second Lieutenants Arthur "Doc" Fielder and Chester T Namola, they were bound for the Moruya gunnery range on the south coast of New South Wales when they became lost in fog. Namola made a forced landing near Berridale, while Fielder force landed on a coastal sandbar at Aslings Beach near Eden. Takala and Musial both perished when their aircraft crashed near Eden, possibly following a mid-air collision.

There was a fourth fatality, this time an Australian civilian caught up in an accident. Eighteen-year-old Daphne Woods died, while a six-year-old child, John Hogan, was badly injured. Second Lieutenant Joseph H King was part of a ferry flight of seven P-40s on 9 March when poor weather forced the flight off course. Short of fuel they landed in a small field. After being refuelled, six of the aircraft took off the next morning. However, King hit a soft spot on the field:

… throwing the aircraft out of control. He ploughed along a fence … & smashed right into a young girl, a younger boy & their pony. The girl was killed instantly, as was the pony and the boy was seriously hurt … [King] … was pretty well broken up … he went to the hospital, saw that the kid was getting along OK, and returned to the drome.

Wurtsmith immediately ordered him back in the air:

… Joe did it, but his crew chief told me … that [he] was shaking like a leaf …

So frustrating were the accidents in light of the urgent need for aircraft and the inexperience of pilots, that Lieutenant-General George H Brett released a message to the Adjutant General in Washington on 5 March:

CITE AGS 620. TWO WIRRAWAYS SIMILAR TO AT DASH SIX AIRCRAFT HAVE BEEN OBTAINED FROM THE AUSTRALIANS FOR EACH PURSUIT SQUADRON (.) THESE WERE OBTAINED FOR TRANSITION TRAINING OF PURSUIT PILOTS (.) THESE PILOTS ARRIVED IN THIS COUNTRY WITHOUT HAVING FLOWN FOR OVER TWO MONTHS AND OVER 75% OF THESE PILOTS HAVE ONLY A FEW HOURS OR NO TIME AT ALL IN P DASH FORTYS (.) SPECIFIC EXAMPLES (.)…NINETY FIVE OF THE ONE HUNDRED AND TWO PILOTS OF THE FORTY NINTH PURSUIT GROUP HAVE NEVER BEEN IN A PURSUIT AIRPLANE (.) THE NUMBER OF WIRRAWAYS FOR TRANSITION TRAINING OBTAINABLE IS ENTIRLEY INSUFFICIENT (.)… THESE PILOTS HAVE BEEN GIVEN AS MUCH TRANSITION AND TRAINING AS POSSIBLE UNDER THE CLOSEST SUPERVISION AND CONTROL OF THE MOST EXPERIENCED AVAILABLE OFFICERS (.) IN SPITE OF THIS THE NUMBER OF ACCIDENTS HAS REACHED EXCESSIVE AND ALARMING PROPORTIONS (.) MOST ACCIDENTS ARE DUE ENTIRELY TO PILOT ERROR (.) DURING THE LAST WEEK FIFTEEN P DASH FORTY AIRCRAFT HAVE BEEN DAMAGED TO THE EXTENT OF NEEDING MAJOR REPAIRS (.) URGENTLY REQUEST THIS SITUATION BE GIVEN THE GREATEST CONSIDERATION (.) LENGTH OF TIME OFF PILOTING DUE TRAVEL SHOULD BE REDUCED TO MINIMUM (.) BETTER TRAINEE PILOTS MUST BE ASSIGNED THIS THEATRE (.) BRETT

Even as the accidents continued, the 49th Pursuit Group was considered operational. On 3 March a 25 aircraft detachment was sent to Melbourne to provide cover for a convoy. This was in response to intelligence reports indicating a Japanese battle group, including an aircraft carrier, was operating in southern waters.

Even that mission was marred by accidents. Clyde Barnett nearly crashed while landing, while Second Lieutenants Ben Duke and "Doc" Fielder, along with Line Chief Sergeant "Pop" Marlin, got lost in an accompanying Wirraway. Landing in a field they finally reached Laverton in the dark. Second Lieutenant Pierre L Alford nosed his P-40 over, Second Lieutenant William Herbert's machine collided with Van Auken's aircraft, John Roth nosed over and Keith Brown selected his undercarriage "up" before take-off.

Led by their CO, Van Auken, the pilots flew daily patrols before returning to Fairbairn on 6

March. During this flight Second Lieutenants Richard E Dennis and Monroe D Eisenberg were driven off course by smoke from bush fires. Short of fuel, they forced landed near Braidwood in New South Wales. Dennis ran into a clump of trees, while Eisenberg skidded through a fence.

Then Captain Allison W Strauss, a veteran of the Philippines campaign, was assigned as commanding officer of the 8th Pursuit Squadron. Strauss was among a number of veteran pilots with P-40 combat experience in the Philippines and/or Java who was assigned to the 49th PG at this time. The group comprised Captain Walter L Coss and First Lieutenants Nathaniel H Blanton, George E Kiser, Jack D Dale and Joseph J Kruzel. Second Lieutenants William J Hennon, Robert B Dockstader, Lester J Johnsen, James B Morehead and Andrew J Reynolds completed the list. Mechanic Joe Cunningham wrote:

> We got more planes and more old pilots, and do they look rugged. They have been in combat already.

The new arrivals added valuable combat experience to the Group. On 19 March, Wurtsmith reported to USAFIA:

> Officer pilots and non pilots [sic] respectively by squadron follows. Hqrs and Hqrs Squadron 5 pilots and 13 non pilots. Seventh Pursuit Squadron 33 pilots and 4 non pilots eight pursuit squadron [sic] 33 pilots and 4 non pilots. Ninth Pursuit Squadron 32 pilots and 4 non pilots. 49 Interceptor Control Squadron no pilots and 3 non pilots.

Wurtsmith also signed off on the allocation of P-40s to the three squadrons, the 43rd Air Materiel Squadron and an initial allocation to the RAAF. Wurtsmith's Memorandum was received at USAFIA HQ on 16 March detailing a total of 113 aircraft.

By this time the 7th and 8th Pursuit Squadrons were preparing to leave Bankstown and Fairbairn. The 9th Pursuit Squadron aircraft were in Darwin while the enlisted men and squadron equipment were en route.

In late March an accounting of the aircraft classified as being "damaged beyond local repair facilities" was undertaken before assigning them to No. 5 Aircraft Depot at RAAF Wagga Wagga. At Williamtown seven aircraft were listed, while at Bankstown there were four and at Fairbairn five. One other was at Laverton while one was listed at Horn Island, far to the north off the tip of Cape York. This aircraft was #41-5313 *Poopy* of the 7th PS, the first of the 49th PG squadrons to see combat over Australia.

Into combat and on to Darwin

Lying off the tip of Queensland's Cape York, Horn Island was the last stop for aircraft flying north to Port Moresby in New Guinea. When the Japanese captured Rabaul in January 1942 the role of Horn Island was heightened, as Port Moresby came under air attack and Horn Island was a relatively safe dispersal area. However as Japanese air activity over New Guinea was stepped up, Allied headquarters decided to detach a fighter unit to Horn Island to intercept any potential raids.

On 4 March Lieutenant Colonel Wurtsmith asked the 7th PS CO, Captain Bob Morrissey, if his unit could provide a detachment for Horn Island. Able to comply, Morrissey led a dozen P-40s from Bankstown on 7 March. Each aircraft had a small tool kit including spark plugs, while the pilots had been instructed on basic aircraft servicing. Only nine of the fighters eventually made it. Two pilots and machines returned south with mechanical problems, while Second Lieutenant Don Lee Jr was left behind. Once at Horn Island the detachment flew daily patrols in preparation for meeting an attack.

On 14 March eight Betty bombers of the No. 4 *Kokutai*, led by Lieutenant Shigeo Yamagata, joined up with 12 Zeros from the same unit, led by Lieutenant Shiro Kawai. At 1215 the Bettys reached Horn Island and released their bombs. Ten minutes later they were attacked by Morrissey's P-40s. In the ensuing combat the Japanese lost two Zeros, though the Americans claimed one Betty and four Zeros. Both Lieutenant Nobohiro Iwasaki and FPO1c Genkichi Oishi were brought down, the former to Captain Morrissey.

Oishi was spotted by Second Lieutenant AT House, who decided on a radical approach:

> I squeezed the trigger and found my guns did not fire, so I continued ... directly at the enemy aircraft, expecting to get his fuselage in the heavy part of my wing. He had started firing, but ... changed course ... the leading edge of my right wing went through his fuselage approximately in the middle of his canopy.

With two feet of his starboard wing missing and the aileron not working, House managed to land the damaged aircraft at Horn Island. There it sat for some time awaiting transport to No. 5

The airfield at Horn Island was little more than a refuelling station. Captain Morrisey's detachment of P-40s lacked any maintenance facilities bar a few tools that the pilots carried themselves.

Aircraft Depot at Wagga. The fighter was eventually returned to service only to be lost in combat over Melville Island on 13 June 1942.

The Americans lost one aircraft in the fight, that of Second Lieutenant Clarence Sanford. The P-40 had been grounded with mechanical problems. Despite this, Sanford took off and after firing on one Zero, he was set upon by two others before losing them in cloud. Disoriented, Sanford flew west before running short of fuel and parachuting into the sea off Bremer Island in far east Arnhem Land – some hundreds of miles from Horn Island. Following an exhausting swim, Sanford struggled ashore. He later wrote:

> I remember feeling the bottom ... and crawling up on the beach – then I fainted.

Discovered by two Aboriginal youths, one of whom was named Wandjuk Marika, Sanford was taken to the mainland and Yirrkala Mission. Sunburnt, suffering cuts, abrasions and swollen feet, Sanford related:

> ... [when] we finally reached the mission I was about finished. The missionary doctored my burns and gave me food. I was in bed there some time and was picked up by mission lugger ... and taken to another mission ... toward Darwin. I was taken out of there by Hudson bomber ... [to] Darwin.

Sanford spent 11 weeks in hospital in Brisbane and a further four months of recovery at Walter Reed Hospital in the US, before being assigned, ironically, as an instructor in survival techniques.

With no accompanying mechanics and with the pilots having to service their own aircraft therewere bound to be problems with the Horn Island detachment. Morrisey reported:

> Only one gun of my P-40 was in working condition ... after taking off I immediately landed and cleared the jams.

Lieutenant William A Redington had the same problem. Following the combat Morrissey reported tersely that

> ... missions cannot be successfully carried out without efficient mechanics, armorers and radio men to maintain the ships. The actual flying of the airplane in combat is enough to keep the pilot busy without having to recharge his guns.

The day following the Horn Island raid a memorandum advised that:

> The 49th Pursuit Group has been ordered to the Darwin Area. The 9th Squadron ... is now en route Williamtown to Darwin. Headquarters and Headquarters Squadron and the 7th Pursuit Squadron is at Bankstown and the 8th Squadron is at Canberra ... will be ready to move on March 24th.

The squadrons prepared for a move as early as 4 March. Joe Cunningham wrote of the 8th PS:

> We are getting ready to ship out ... all we did today was pack a few things and clean the hangers. (sic)

The wreckage of Guinea Airways Lockheed Super Electra VH-ADY is gathered for inspection at Annaburoo Station. Ten enlisted members of the 49th PG's Interceptor Control Squadron lost their lives in the crash, in addition to the two Guinea Airways pilots. (State Library of South Australia)

On 6 March Second Lieutenant Frederick F Hollier and a crew of 9th PS enlisted men left Sydney aboard a Qantas flying boat bound for Darwin. The following day Second Lieutenant Robert McComsey and a group of enlisted men left by Douglas DC-3. The main party travelled by train before boarding a convoy of trucks to across the inhospitable Barkly Tableland from Mount Isa, and on to Larrimah before entraining for Batchelor airfield. Ralph Boyce was among the lucky few travelling by air:

> At long last I'm off to the front! ... I'm seated comfortably in a Douglas DC-3 ... next stop in about 10 hours will be Darwin or thereabouts.

Instead the DC-3 stopped at Daly Waters overnight as:

> ... the pilot decided it would be unwise to come in [to Batchelor] after dark as the AA crews have an unpleasant habit of taking pot shots at planes ... We took off again at 4:00 AM, reaching ... Batchelor Field ... about 7 [AM]. Here we found ... our squadron set up in a wilderness home some mile or so from the main field.

For the men of the Interceptor Control Squadron there was little difference in their move north, though they were held up in Brisbane for two weeks before the move by air and ground convoy. Not all made it to Darwin. On 21 April a Lockheed Super 14 airliner, VH-ADY *Adelaide*, took off from Archerfield bound for Batchelor. Chartered from Guinea Airways the aircraft was flown by two experienced Guinea Airways pilots, Captain Gordon Cameron and First Officer William T Gray, with ten enlisted men aboard.

The aircraft become lost in stormy weather, and with poor communications they overflew Batchelor and Darwin and were not heard from again. No further trace of the aircraft or its

In the immediate weeks after the 19 February raid there was no fighter defence at Darwin and Japanese aircraft could overfly the town with relative impunity. This photo was taken by a C5M Babs reconnaissance aircraft on 4 March, with the Darwin RAAF base visible on the lower left.

occupants was found, despite widespread searches, until 25 June, when the burnt-out wreckage of the airliner was found by a station owner while mustering cattle.

The 9th PS only had to wait until 22 March when it scored the first victory for the 49th PG. A reconnaissance of the Darwin area was carried out by a C5M Babs crewed by FPO1c Shigiki Mori and FPO1c Shinobu Nagasawa, escorted by three Zeros of the No. 3 *Kokutai* led by Lieutenant Takeo Kurosawa. The survey of the area was short-lived when the Babs and Zeros separated and P-40s of the 9th PS struck. The Babs was intercepted and shot down over the Port Patterson area by Second Lieutenants Clyde L Harvey and Stephen Poleschuk at 20,000 feet. Poleschuk reported:

> … we sighted one Nakajima, Type 97 [sic]. I do not think our approach was observed. I delivered a 30 [degree] beam attack at less than 200 feet [and] … fired one hundred rounds. The enemy made a 180 [degree] diving turn to left and then a shallow climbing turn to right … and was shot down in flames.

Clyde Harvey's report was brief:

> … We sighted a Nakajima Serial #3 [sic] at 19,000 feet. I made a diving attack on the enemy and he started a steep turn. The Nakajima started burning and pilot jumped in chute. We then returned to our base.

Following the toss of a coin Poleschuk was awarded the "kill". Both of the Babs crew died and their bodies were not recovered. The Americans had noted the fixed undercarriage of their victim but had seemingly mis-identified it as a single-seat Type 97 fighter, the obsolete Nakajima Ki-27 as used by the Japanese Army.

A Zero pilot by the name of Tokaji (not Lieutenant Tadatsune Tokaji, who was killed on 23 August 1942) is reported as failing to return to base following the action of 22 March, but no reports of combat with the escorting Zeros are included in the combat reports of Harvey or Poleschuk. However, the No. 3 *Ku Kodochosho* records only the loss of one aircraft of the four involved in the mission. The possibility exists that Tokaji crashed due to mechanical problems *en route* to Koepang following the Darwin attack.

Meanwhile, 200 miles to the south of and inland from Darwin, the small town of Katherine was attacked, unprotected by fighter cover, by nine Bettys of the Takao *Kokutai*, after an initial undetected overflight by a Babs. It was also the day that the radar of No. 31 RDF station finally came online at Dripstone Cliffs north of Darwin. An RAAF mechanic at the site, John Scott, recalled that:

> … the first enemy aircraft were located at a distance of 80 miles … the crew on watch were Bill Wellstead, mechanic, Fred Findlay and Kevin Wass, operators, with Fred Findlay being on the cathode ray tube.

The Katherine raid, however, was undetected by the radar operators. At the Katherine target area Lieutenant Colonel Ralph C Glover of the recently arrived US 808th Engineer Battalion reported:

> At approximately 1330 [hours] the sound of planes flying at high altitude over Katherine could be heard. Their engines made a particular high pitched noise. They were finally spotted. There were nine silver colored planes flying in perfect V formation at an altitude of approximately 20,000 feet … [they] flew in a straight line westward until they disappeared … In about 15 or 20 minutes they could be heard approaching again at about the same altitude and flew eastward on the same bearing until they again disappeared from view.

Indeed, after overflying Katherine from the northeast the formation had turned and headed back in about 15 or 20 minutes. They circled three times – something never done in later times when there was possible opposition, and one pass over the target became the rule. On one of the passes the aircraft were seen to release a balloon, which would have been used to calculate the prevailing winds and their effect on the ordnance descent. At 1227 the Bettys released their bombs over the aerodrome at 20,000 feet.

Most of the bombs landed on the aerodrome, though one also landed near the Gallon Licence Store leaving a crater and shrapnel damage. An Aboriginal man, 42-year old Dodger Kajalwal, was sheltering behind a rock near the store where he was hit and killed by shrapnel. A local man, Noel Hall, was also injured when one of his fingers was severed by shrapnel while another Aboriginal man, Hector, was also injured by shrapnel. Both were treated at the 121st Australian General Hospital.

Turning for home after the release of their bombs the Bettys were unhindered during their return trip and landed back at Koepang at 1620.

Following the raid, military personnel and a group of PMG linesmen who had also witnessed the raid, inspected the aerodrome and assessed the damage. They noted that:

On further examination ... about 85 bomb craters of varying sizes were located. The holes were well scattered all over. If there had been any planes on the taxiway system, they would have undoubtedly been destroyed.

A fine study of 7th Pursuit Squadron P-40s over typical Northern Territory terrain, over which the American pilots were quick to familiarise themselves in early 1942. (Bob Alford)

A C5M Babs reconnaissance aircraft, distinguishable by its long greenhouse-style canopy and fixed spatted undercarriage. One of these aircraft was downed near Darwin on 22 March, just days after the arrival of first 49th PG P-40s in the northern town. (Michael Claringbould)

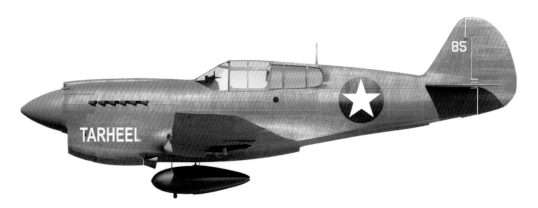

The P-40E named Tarheel of Second Lieutenant George E Preddy, who was a member of the 9th Fighter Squadron's "Dragon Flight" before being badly injured in a mid-air collision. (Michael Claringbould)

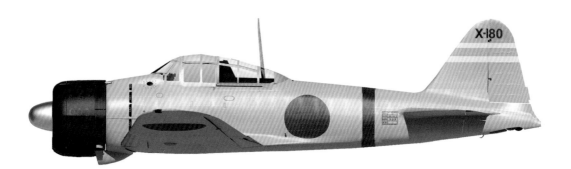

An A6M2 Type 21 Zero of the No. 3 Kokutai as based in Timor in 1942. The fin and fuselage stripes denoted flight leaders within the unit and were used for visual orientation by the pilots who did not normally carry radios. (Michael Claringbould)

CHAPTER 5

The Opponents: the P-40 versus the Zero and the Betty

With the arrival of the 49th PG in Darwin in late March 1942, the scene was set for the air campaign which would unfold over the coming months. The P-40Es used by the Americans would repeatedly try and intercept incoming raids by IJN Betty bombers escorted by A6M2 Zero fighters. How did these different aircraft compare and what were their strengths and weaknesses?

The P-40 and the Zero

In some ways both the P-40 and the Zero were broadly comparable. Both were monoplanes developed from the late 1930s with retractable undercarriages and a tailwheel. The two aircraft both had powerful engines driving multiblade propellers in front of the pilot. Both had metal skins all-around and had the pilot sitting under a sliding canopy with good visibility. However, the P-40's cockpit design was faired into the rear fuselage which obscured rearwards vision.

Regarding fuel usage, the heavier weight of the P-40 meant it burnt more fuel, especially when making maximum speed climbs. As virtually all of the 1942 combats began after such climbs, the 49th PG pilots had a tight window in which to engage in combat at full power before needing to disengage and return to base. The light weight of the Zero gave it an extraordinary combat range which enabled escort missions to be flown such as those against Darwin. Such missions over Japanese territory were well beyond the capabilities of the P-40. Both the P-40 and the Zero used drop tanks which were jettisoned prior to combat.

Name	Country	Armament	Top Speed/Weight	Engine	Combat Radius
Curtiss P-40E Kittyhawk / Warhawk	USA	6 x 0.50-inch machine guns in wings	334 mph at 14,000 feet 8,515 lb (loaded)	1,240hp Allison V-1710-39 in-line	200 miles
Mitsubishi A6M2 Zero	Japan	2 x 20mm cannon in wings 2 x 7.7mm machine guns in engine cowling	331 mph at 14,930 feet 6,164 lb (loaded)	950hp Nakajima Sakae 12 air-cooled radial	600 miles

The Zero could out-climb a P-40, and the Zero performed slightly better at height given its lower wing loading. Conversely the P-40 could out dive the Zero and could withstand higher G forces when pulling out of a high-speed dive. However, the Zero was a better dogfighter. Patrick Masell summarises:

The overall performance of the A6M Zero and the P-40 Warhawk were as different as night and day. While the P-40 employed speed and survivability, the Zero relied on its tight turn-radius and swift climb to succeed in combat. The A6M's nimbleness was legendary; in low-speed dogfights it almost guaranteed success.

The Americans first learnt how to fight the Zero with the P-40 in China under Claire Chennault, an ex-US Army captain who had formed a squadron of volunteer US pilots to fight for the Chinese government. The aviators, trained in Chennault's fighting techniques, achieved an outstanding combat record using height to pounce on Zeros which they had been warned by radio were coming:

> The Curtiss was sturdy, fast and stable. Stable is good, except in a dogfight. The Zero, on the other hand, was highly manoeuvrable, fast and light. Light is good, except when you get hit by enemy gunfire. The Zero was very vulnerable to a hit. If you could just hit the Zero once, you could most likely bring it down. But, to bring down the P-40, you had to hit it a lot; like the prize fighter who can take punches.

Lieutenant Commander Kofukuda, flight commander of the IJN No. 6 *Kokutai* which fought over Guadalcanal, accurately recorded at the time that the manoeuvrability of the American P-40 was markedly inferior to the Zero:

> While the Tomahawk [sic] possessed the same maximum speed as the [Zero], it lacked the rate of climb of our fighter and could not hope to match it in close combat. The Tomahawk pilots therefore took advantage of their superior diving speed, and almost invariably resorted to "shoot and retreat" tactics. Thus, they usually refused combat unless they possessed the advantage of altitude, which enabled them to dive into the [Zero] formations with blazing guns and race away at a diving speed beyond that possible with a [Zero].

In terms of reliability both types of aircraft functioned well in 1942, when the Japanese were yet to face the logistical limitations which they faced in the latter part of the Pacific War. However, the P-40 was never designed as an interceptor and its supercharger only gave maximum performance below 15,000 feet. This meant that the American machine was decidedly sluggish in high altitude combats.

A major advantage of the P-40 in the harsh northern Australian environment was its ability to take punishment, especially as compared to the lightly built Zero. This was well illustrated in the preceding chapter when a 7th PS P-40 rammed a Zero over Horn Island. While the Japanese aircraft disintegrated in a shower of debris the American pilot was able to land his badly damaged aircraft.

Naval officer Nat Gould flew both RAF Hurricanes in Russia and RAAF Kittyhawks in Milne Bay. After his first Kittyhawk flight, he wrote:

> Don't like them: too heavy, no climb, no manoeuvrability.

He changed his mind after Milne Bay when he found his "bulldozer with wings" took and delivered more punishment than even his rugged Hurricane:

One Kittyhawk returned to Milne Bay with a hole just forward of the tail big enough to put your head through. That would have destroyed a Hurricane.

The P-40 also had self-sealing fuel tanks and pilot armour whereas the Zero did not. A hit in the area of the tanks or pilot could therefore prove devastating. These factors, together with a lack of durability, proved to be serious shortcomings for the Japanese fighter. In comparison, the P-40 was much more of an all-round performer as summarised in the following table:

	A6M2 Zero	P-40E Warhawk
Performance		
Climbing	Excellent	Lesser
Diving	Lesser	Excellent
Manoeuvrability	Excellent	Lesser
Fuel usage	Excellent	Lesser
Wing loading	Excellent	Lesser
Acceleration	Excellent	Lesser
Speed	Lesser	Fair
Ease of use	Excellent	Fair
Design		
Armament	Lighter machineguns and slow firing cannon	Excellent heavy machineguns
Durability	Poor	Excellent
Undercarriage	Very strong	Reasonable
Pilot armour	Non-existent	Present
Pilot visibility	Excellent	Obscured at rear
Self-sealing fuel tanks	Non-existent	Present

A final note about the Zeros over Darwin in 1942 concerns their parent unit, the No. 3 *Kokutai*. It had only been formed as a fighter unit a short time before the start of the Pacific War, however most of its pilots had experienced combat over China. Between December 1941 and March 1942, No. 3 *Ku* saw extensive action over the Philippines and the Netherlands East Indies and destroyed scores of Allied aircraft in return for only modest losses of its own. Hence at the start of the 1942 Darwin air campaign the No. 3 *Ku* was an elite fighting unit whose pilots were vastly more experienced than those of the 49th PG.

The Betty Bomber

The Mitsubishi G4M1 Betty was a land-based bomber used by the Japanese Naval Air Force. It was perhaps the best-known Japanese bomber of the war, in its four main types. In December 1941 it was still quite a new design, with only 120 in service, having succeeded the G3M1 (code-named "Nell" by the Allies). Two months later, Bettys made up half of the high-level twin-engine bombers – Nells the other half – that attacked Darwin in the second raid of 19 February 1942. From then on, the G3M1 Betty was the bomber which featured the most in the combat flights – over 200 in total – which were made against targets in northern Australia and off its coast. The bombing raids against Darwin during the 1942 dry season were all conducted by the Takao *Kokutai*, operating from bases in the NEI.

Mitsubishi G4M1 Betty Specifications	
2 x 1,530hp engines	Speed: 231mph max; 196mph cruise
Range: 2,315 nautical miles loaded	Weight: 21,000 lb (loaded)
Crew: 7	
Armament: 4 x 7.7mm Type 92 MGs (nose, dorsal blister, L & R beam blisters); 1 x 20mm Type 99 cannon (tail); plus up to approximately 2,200lb of bombs or a single torpedo.	

The Betty was a low wing monoplane with twin engines, slung in mid-section on the aircraft wing. Because of the design of the rear gun position, the fuselage did not taper in the normal way, but remained almost cylindrical throughout its entire length. This led to the aircraft gaining the nickname of *hamaki* (cigar).

The G4M1 was designed to bomb targets at a range of 1,000-1,500 miles. Allied bombers flying missions of comparable length were large aircraft with four engines: B-17s and B-24s. These weighed, fully loaded, over 50,000 pounds as opposed to two engines and an all up weight of 21,000 pounds for the Betty. Weight saving measures included that when loaded with bombs, the bomb-bay doors were permanently removed, only being attached for ferry or training flights. The Mitsubishi designers made many compromises to ensure the G4M1 was light enough to preserve its long-range capability with just two engines. G4M1s could attack targets at what were regarded as extreme ranges in early 1942, appearing without warning from any direction.

A G4M1 Betty bomber of the Takao Kokutai in 1942, still wearing an early China period camouflage scheme. Note the exposed bombs in the absence of bomb bay doors. The red hinomaru on the fuselage was painted over a circular door of almost the exact same size. (Michael Claringbould)

Bombing from medium to high altitudes, Betty bombers were out of range of most ground defences and were usually quick enough to get away before the defenders could react. Fighters had a hard time chasing the fast bombers at altitude, and if they did catch them the 20mm cannon in the tail of the G4M1s was a powerful deterrent. These tactics worked perfectly when Takao *Kokutai* G4M1s first attacked targets in northern Australia.

The weapons used to defend the Betty were not the best. Although the tail cannon was formidable, the armament used in the dorsal, waist and nose positions was insufficient. These positions were equipped with 7.7mm machine guns similar to the famous First World War Lewis light machine gun. These light weapons performed poorly as compared to the far heavier 0.50-inch calibre machine guns used in US bombers. The 7.7mm round couldn't penetrate armour plate and lacked destructive power to cause serious damage to rugged Allied airframes such as that of the P-40.

Another defensive aspect of the Betty was that it had no armour protection for the crew and no self-sealing wing fuel cells. This meant that if the wing tanks were struck by bullets there was a substantial risk of fire, especially given the red-hot engines operating nearby.

The Betty's willingness to catch fire was not known at first: its operations in China were successful due to a combination of bombing from height, defensive formation discipline and capable fighter escorts. But eventually the bombers acquired the nickname of "One-Shot Lighter" from the Allies due to this characteristic.

The aircraft fire extinguishers were inadequate, and when 5mm armour plate was fitted around the tail cannon it was so ineffective it was often removed in the field. In addition, the aircrews usually did not take parachutes with them, showing a willingness to operate the aircraft until destruction – an attitude both admirable and foolish:

> …one thing they would not do was bail out over enemy territory. In a conspicuous decision to forsake this option, the men of the land attack corps carried no parachutes on combat missions. All too often, in the thick of the fight, a final wave to salute from a burning cockpit was the last anyone would see of a seven-man team on its final plunge.

Overall the Bettys gave good service over Darwin in 1942, but would prove vulnerable at times when flying too low or without a hefty escort of Zeros.

A busy scene at Koepang, where No. 3 Ku Zeros equipped with drop tanks prepare for a mission against Darwin. Note their tail codes have been obscured by the wartime censor. A single Takao Ku Betty passes overhead. (Bob Alford)

CHAPTER 6

The First Combats: March-May 1942

When the first elements of the 49th PG arrived in Darwin, the RAAF had its own fighter control unit know as No. 5 Fighter Sector, which operated from tents to the south of the RAAF base in what was known as "Sandfly Gully". This was linked to the first RDF station which was only just being calibrated and was untested in operations, as Second Lieutenant Jesse Peaslee reported:

> …the air raid warning system was still pretty much in the theoretical stage …[RDF] was supposed to give an 80-mile warning, but … it was often not functioning … The firing of anti-aircraft guns was often the only warning of an impending air raid.

From March 1942, a small RAAF group established an observation post on Bathurst Island, north of Cape Fourcroy. Led by acting Corporal Bill Woodnutt, the group included two airmen and a couple of local Tiwi Islanders, with their bush camp established near Wiyaparaly which meant "the place of the big sand dune". They passed information to No. 5 Fighter Sector through callsign 8X7. The post was ideally situated, with Cape Fourcroy being something of a focal point:

> … the Japanese used [it] as a navigational point, every raid passed virtually overhead … the unit counted the number of planes passing and after contacting 5FS they waited to hear details of the raid.

Lieutenant Colonel Wurtsmith later wrote to Air Commodore Frank "Pop" Bladin, the Air Officer Commanding North Western Area (NWA) praising:

> … the excellent performance of the W/T crew stationed at Cape Fourcroy, Bathurst Island … On the first day of operation the messages received were letter perfect … this station had definitely proven its value and Acting Corporal Woodnutt and his crew are to be commended.

By 26 March still only one squadron had arrived in Darwin, the 9th PS which could boast 17 serviceable P-40s and 28 pilots. Two days later four of its P-40s intercepted seven Bettys of the Takao *Ku* led by Lieutenant Takeji Fujiwara. The target was the Darwin RAAF base. Armed with 83 x 60-kilogram bombs the raiders were over Darwin at 1445. They released the bombs from 18,000 feet, damaging one Wirraway and cratering the runway.

The P-40s intercepted the bombers as they exited Darwin to the northwest. Piloting the fighters were Second Lieutenants Mitchell Zawisza, Clyde L Harvey, Robert H Vaught and William D Sells. Harvey followed his prey seven miles out over the ocean, and then downed the Betty of Lieutenant Taketoshi Asihiro and his crew:

> I first saw enemy bombers at 19,000 feet … and followed them … out to sea … [I] dived

down on one from the rear, and was shot at …[so] I dived, came up under his belly, and let him have a short burst and he burst into flame.

The plaudits came quickly. Headquarters NWA relayed congratulations from Air Chief Marshal Sir Charles Burnett, Chief of the Air Staff, RAAF to all concerned:

Quote. Please … RD/F personnel and P40 pilots for effective interception 28/3. Tails up. Unquote.

The same day saw Cypher Message 2342 from HQ USAFIA to the three squadrons directing that:

The red circle in the American insignia on all aeroplanes will be immediately painted white. Purpose is to avoid our aircraft being mistaken for enemy aircraft particularly by ground troops. All Australian military forces will be advised of this change.

In reality many of the fighter aircraft had already had the red centre either painted out or reduced in size from as early as February.

The Takao *Ku* bombers soon returned on consecutive days at the end of the month. Led by Lieutenant Yoshinobu Kusuhata, a force of seven Bettys escorted by 12 Zeros, led by Lieutenant Takeo Kurosawa, attacked the RAAF base on 30 March. Armed with 42 x 60-kilogram and seven 250-kilogram bombs, the Bettys departed Koepang at 1200 in company with the escorting Zeros. They approached Darwin at 16,000 feet and released the bombs at 1445. However, the raid caused only slight damage to the runway as most bombs fell into the adjoining bush.

As they exited Darwin, several P-40s attempted to intercept the Bettys, however the Zeros were quick to protect the bombers. Second Lieutenant James L Porter had the tail of his aircraft shot up. Second Lieutenant William D Sells' aircraft was also damaged, and Second Lieutenant Robert M McComsey was forced to bail out when his aircraft stalled over Darwin harbour. Landing safely under his parachute in a mangrove-lined inlet in the southern reaches of the port, he was rescued and returned to his unit. Like so many aircraft from the war, his aircraft went into the sea and has never been found.

The RAAF station was attacked again the following day by seven Bettys led by Lieutenant Takeji Fujiwara. The escort was eight Zeros and a Babs reconnaissance aircraft led by Lieutenant Toshitada Kawazoe. The Babs departed Koepang for an early reconnaissance of Darwin with the Bettys and Zeros following. The raiding force approached the target at 17,000 feet and released 4,270 kilograms of bombs at 1252, destroying 20 drums of fuel and causing slight damage to the runways.

Five P-40s intercepted the force, but despite some damage inflicted there were no losses despite claims by both sides. Second Lieutenant Andrew J Reynolds was credited with one Betty and the anti-aircraft batteries claimed another. In actuality, as the Japanese records show, there were no losses to the raiding force. On their part, the Japanese claimed three P-40s destroyed and two probables, but there were no losses there either. The overclaiming and crediting of questionable aerial victories over the Darwin area by both sides had commenced in earnest.

Soldiers inspecting the wreckage of a Betty at Nightcliff beach which was shot down by AA fire on 4 April 1942.

That evening the first night raid against Darwin was flown when three Bettys led by Lieutenant Yoshinobu Kusuhata targeted the RAAF base, although no damage was reported. It would be the last night attack until July, when the Japanese switched to mainly night raids.

The first of five raids during April 1942 came on the second day of the month when seven Bettys, led by Lieutenant Takeji Fujiwara, and escorted by three Zeros, targeted the town, the naval Oil Fuel Installation on Stokes Hill and the nearby Shell fuel depot. The bombs fell in a line through the town with damage to homes and the loss of 30,000 gallons of fuel oil at the Shell depot. The AA batteries at the Darwin Oval and at Berrimah engaged the bombers with 16 x 3.7" AA rounds, while 16 P-40s were scrambled and intercepted the Bettys but there were no losses to either side. The 9th PS mechanics had a catch-up day of maintenance the following day, while ground staff settled in after arriving in Darwin on 31 March.

The next raid came on 4 April and was a day of mixed fortunes for the 9th PS. Six Bettys led by Lieutenant Yoshinobu Kusuhata, escorted by six Zeros, attacked the Darwin RAAF station and the civil aerodrome at Parap. Approaching Darwin at 22,000 feet they were intercepted by seven scrambled P-40s. However, they were not successful in preventing the bombers reaching their target. At 1353 the two three-aircraft elements flying in a V formation released their combined total of 3,660 kilograms of bombs.

Three Bettys were downed. One was hit by AA fire and crashed into the Nightcliff foreshore, while one was shot down over the Cox Peninsula and the third went down into the sea. The Bettys had two seven-man and one eight-man crew, piloted by FCPO Noboru Ashazawa, Flyer1c Shigeoshi Matsuda and Flyer1c Denichi Inada. All 22 men were killed.

While the Japanese claimed to have downed four P-40s, two were victims of friendly fire from the AA guns. Second Lieutenants Grover J Gardner and John D Livingstone flew over the RAAF station with their wheels lowered as the signal for the day. Fired on by nervous ground defences, both were hit. Gardner bailed out over Cox Peninsula and was rescued, while Livingstone, badly wounded, flew to the 34-Mile airstrip where, as the 9th PS CO, Captain Jim Selman recalled, he was:

> Killed on the South overrun…he was burned and still sitting in the cockpit when I found him. He was buried in Darwin Cemetery.

Following the war, as was the case with all US graves that could be found, Livingstone's body was disinterred and returned to home territory.

The 9th PS pilots claimed – and were credited with downing – seven of the six Bettys and two Zeros, while the Fannie Bay AA battery claimed two of the bombers. Second Lieutenant Andrew J Reynolds, a veteran of the ill-fated Java campaign, reported seeing four bombers and two Zeros shot down. Reynolds, John D Landers, Gardner, John A Kelting and John S Sauber were credited with one Betty and one Zero, two Bettys, one Betty, one Betty, and one Zero respectively.

The wreckage of the Betty which crashed on the Cox Peninsula was recovered and it was identified as having the tail-code T-361. Second Lieutenant Landers reported that he had:

> … sighted enemy bombers - two close, one straggler and one Zero at 20,000 feet. We attacked … [and] … this pilot shot down one straggling bomber.

Second Lieutenant John D Livingstone's wrecked P-40 at the 34-Mile strip, just after it crashed on 4 April 1942. The strip was later named Livingstone Field in his honour.

Reports confirm Landers watched it breaking up over Cox Peninsula, strongly suggesting it was Betty T-361. The second-in-command of West Point battery, Lieutenant Cyril Molyneux, recalled the crash:

> The main fuselage was fairly intact, one engine nearby, the other missing. One body outside plane and two inside. There may have been a fourth. I took personal papers from the body inside including photos (no doubt of his family) and sent these across to Darwin.

On 5 April, seven Bettys led by Lieutenant Takeji Fujiwara, and nine Zeros led by Lieutenant Sada-o Yamaguchi, again attacked the Darwin RAAF base. The bombers approached the target at 1150 and two minutes later released 5,040 kilograms of bombs from 24,000 feet, causing only slight damage to the main runway. They were intercepted by four P-40s with no losses to either side, though the Betty crews claimed five Allied aircraft destroyed.

At the time the parent unit to both the Takao and No. 3 *Kokutai*, the 23rd *Koku Sentai* had available 45 Bettys, 45 Zeros and six Babs on strength, with a detachment of the Takao *Ku* still in the Philippines and engaged in operations against Bataan and Corregidor.

Notwithstanding the Philippines detachment, Takao *Ku* had the aircraft available to maintain the pressure on the Darwin defences. However, they failed to do so, and in that missed opportunity the 49th PG was afforded a breathing space which allowed for the arrival of the remaining air and ground personnel. The raid of 5 April was the last in which the 9th PS was to intercept as Darwin's sole aerial defence.

April 1942 – a group united

While the bombing campaign against Darwin continued and the Babs of No. 3 *Ku* maintained their regular reconnaissance missions over the top end, in early April the 49th Pursuit Group was nearing full strength. The 7th PS's P-40s arrived at Batchelor on 9 April following their flight across the outback, while the 8th PS began its move a week later.

Both deployments faced similar problems to those experienced by the 9th PS a month earlier. On 16 April Clyde Barnett and two remaining pilots, Second Lieutenants Monroe Eisenberg and Mitchell "Eck" Sims, departed Fairbairn only to return with generator and hydraulic problems. The next day they reached Williamtown. Poor weather forced them down at Coolangatta and the following day, 18 April, they flew on to Archerfield. From there they flew the so-called "Brereton Route" via Charleville. A day later they arrived at Cloncurry, along with two DC-3s, before reaching Daly Waters in the Northern Territory. The next stop was the Adelaide River airfield, which became their temporary base. They arrived in rain as darkness fell, with Barnett recalling:

> We had been told there was a runway through the anthills so we were very careful ... I landed high and hot but got in OK.

Following the arduous flights across the Brereton Route and simultaneous overland journeys by enlisted personnel, the 49th PG, while scattered between Darwin, Batchelor and Adelaide River, was at least in the combat zone.

Nearer to Darwin permanent airstrips for the 8th and 9th Pursuit Squadrons at the 27- and 34-Mile pegs on the main north-south road were close to completion by the American 808th Engineer Battalion (Aviation) as part of the RAAF's aerodrome development program. These strips were later named Strauss and Livingstone, in honour of deceased 49th PG pilots, and both still may be seen today near the Stuart Highway.

In the meantime, the Takao *Ku* had been operating against northern Australia with only part its available strength, while the remainder was still in the Philippines. However, an intercepted Japanese radio message of 25 April was decoded in part and stated that this detachment was returning to its parent unit at its home base of Kendari in the NEI:

> Heavy bombers of Takao are leaving MA [Manila] at 0800 tomorrow the 26th for #329 base [Kendari] and will fly via #920 base.

Projected numbers for planned raids on 25 and 27 April were also revealed in radio intercepts.

While the bombing campaign against Darwin intensified, reconnaissance sorties were regularly flown by the Babs of No. 3 *Ku*. On 15 April 1942 a Babs, escorted by four Zeros, left Koepang at 0905. They were over Darwin around three hours later at 1155. No interception was made – testimony to the difficulty of detecting such small aircraft in small formations with a warning network that was still gaining experience.

A week later on 22 April another reconnaissance of the RAAF airfield was flown by No. 3 *Ku* when a Babs escorted by four Zeros took off from Koepang at 0904. The aircraft were over Darwin at 1120. Again, with no attempted interception they returned safely to base.

A review of the situation at Koepang, where raids by RAAF Hudsons were becoming more frequent, forced a decision to withdraw the Zeros and Bettys back to Kendari. Koepang would remain in use as a forward staging base. Before the withdrawal, the commander of the 23rd *Koku Sentai*, Rear Admiral Ryuzo Takenaka, ordered a major raid on Darwin for 25 April. This was a highly symbolic date in Australia: Anzac Day.

On 25 April, a Babs flew a pre-strike reconnaissance of the Darwin area followed by the strike force of 27 Bettys led by Lieutenant Commander Goro Katsumi. Three bombers aborted the mission with engine problems, with one forced to ditch in Dili harbour. With an escort of nine Zeros led by Lieutenant Takahide Aioi, the remaining Bettys carried out the attack which caused widespread damage to the RAAF base. Two US Army personnel, both from the 147th Field Artillery Regiment, died as a result of the raid: Captain GE Porter was killed and Captain TJ Rozum died of his injuries the following day.

Damage was widespread. An LP2 Machine Gun Carrier, a jeep and an ammunition truck were destroyed (the LP2 Carrier was the only armoured vehicle destroyed on Australian soil in WWII as a result of enemy activity). Two RAAF Hudsons, the water pipeline paralleling the railway line and telephone lines were damaged.

Flying together for the first time following their arrival in the Darwin area, some 50 P-40s scrambled, although only the 7th and 8th Pursuit Squadrons intercepted the Bettys as they exited Darwin to the northwest. However, such numbers were enough to overwhelm the nine Zero escorts. In a 35-minute running combat extending out to sea one Zero was brought down. The pilot, FPO1c Shiro Murakami, was thought to have been downed by 7th PS pilot, First Lieutenant William Hennon, who caught the Zero some 20 miles northwest of Darwin. Hennon reported:

> One of the Zeros dove, but fired out of range then headed out to sea. I followed him, came up behind and opened fire at 100 feet. He exploded … parts of the destroyed plane struck my ship but caused only minor damage. I saw the Zero falling in six or seven pieces, all in flames.

A formation of Takao Ku Bettys crosses the coastline during their 25 April 1942 Darwin raid. The wartime censor has obscured the tail codes.

Four Bettys were downed by the P-40s, including two credited to Second Lieutenant Lieutenants Clyde Barnett and Richard Dennis, with the loss of 32 crewmen. Twenty of the bombers suffered varying degrees of damage. Three had an engine shot out. Two of the damaged bombers force landed on their return flight to Timor. This action was the most significant victory for the P-40s of the entire campaign, with a total of six Bettys and one Zero lost as a direct result of the combat.

Of the two Bettys that ditched on the return flight, one went in 80 miles from Koepang. The other, flown by a seriously wounded Lieutenant Takeharu Fujiwara, was crippled with 180 bullet holes and the port engine shot out. Four of his crewmen had died, but the wounded Fujiwara managed to belly land the aircraft at Koepang. The remaining aircraft landed at 1330.

Despite the Japanese losses no P-40s were downed. Claims by both sides were exaggerated: the Japanese claimed ten P-40s destroyed while the Americans claimed ten Bettys and three Zeroes. The *Argus* newspaper of 27 April repeated the exaggeration by reporting that the Darwin raid cost the Japanese eight bombers and three fighters. However at least the Allied claims had some basis in fact on this occasion.

Of all the combat reports that day by the inexperienced P-40 pilots, Clyde Barnett's diary describes best the moments following the order to scramble:

> My throat was suddenly dry as a bone and I couldn't swallow. At the same time my stomach heaved and I could taste sour bile in my mouth ... it wasn't till I was at about 5000 ft that I settled down ...

For all his initial nerves, Barnett was awarded a Betty shot down:

> I pulled away from him and watched him burn and crash into the sea ... That was the first time I had ever made a firing pass at an aerial target and I damn nearly ran into him.

Inexperience also showed in the pilots' navigational skills. One force-landed on Bathurst Island

Lieutenant Clyde Barnett in the cockpit of his P-40 named Smiley at the 27-Mile strip in 1942. On 25 April he was credited with shooting down two Betty bombers. (Bob Alford)

while others landed at Batchelor and Pine Creek, both to the south of Darwin. One other pilot, who must have been well and truly lost, landed at Pago Pago near Kalumburu Mission in the remote Kimberley region of Western Australia.

Two days later, on 27 April, the Japanese reappeared over Darwin, commencing with a pre-strike reconnaissance of the Darwin area by a Babs of No. 3 *Ku*. Lieutenant Tanemasa Hirata then led 17 Bettys in an attack on the RAAF base, while 21 Zeros led by Lieutenant Takeo Kurusawa provided escort (more than double the strength of the escort provided two days earlier). At 1135 the bombers released 11,160 kilograms of bombs from 20,000 feet. The AA guns of the Darwin Oval, Fannie Bay and Berrimah batteries fired a total of 141 x 3.7-inch rounds against them. Three RAAF sergeants and a corporal were killed in the attack. Damage was received to the No. 1 Officers' accommodation block, the Airmens' Mess kitchen, the recreation hall, the main North-South Road and the water pipeline.

The 49th PG scrambled three squadrons and following a running battle lost four P-40s and two pilots killed in action. The CO of the 8th PS, Captain Allison W Strauss, a veteran of the Philippines campaign, was shot down and crashed into Fannie Bay while a fellow 8th PS pilot, Second Lieutenant Owen W Fish, was downed over the western side of the harbor. Observers suggested that:

> ...the pilot was still alive when he made a slow roll at 3,000 feet. A motor launch went out immediately and found portions of the plane, an identification card and fragments of a body. The ... card was that of Lt Fish.

Captain Allison W Strauss

Captain Allison W Strauss was born on 25 Mar 1916. From Posey County, Indiana, he was awarded the Purple Heart after his death, and the Silver Star for "for conspicuous gallantry and intrepidity in action during World War II". He is buried at Laurel Hill Cemetery, Wadesville, Posey County, Indiana, USA.

Captain Alison Strauss, who was killed on 27 April 1942.

Second Lieutenant Charles C Johnson had been leading the flight, with Fish as his wingman:

Fish and I started down ... [at] 900 yards from bombers ... [a] burst of tracers coming from behind passed over my right wing and a 20mm shell exploded in my right elevator. Fish yelled, "Look out, Johnnie!" ... [he] must have been hit at the same time that I was fired on, or quite possibly he was trying to protect me ... I owe him plenty.

Captain Allison Strauss was last seen under attack by Zeros, as reported by Second Lieutenant Earl R Kingsley:

Captain Strauss saw the Zero, pumped the stick a couple of times, then turned right in a very tight turn ... [Then] the Zero started firing ...

Two further P-40s were lost. Second Lieutenant Stephen Andrew of the 7th PS was forced to bail out of his damaged aircraft after it was hit over Quail Island. Landing safely under his parachute in the sea, he spent some hours swimming, while four P-40s flew top cover, before he finally made it to the Cox Peninsula. Struggling ashore, coincidentally near another P-40 lying on a reef, he managed to attract the attention of a group of patrolling Australian soldiers and was taken to their camp at the Charles Point lighthouse.

The P-40 aircraft that Second Lieutenant Andrew had seen as he limped ashore was that of Second Lieutenant James H Martin of the 8th PS. He had force landed off Gilruth Point after his engine was damaged in combat. Martin reported:

Throttling back ... the engine ... ran worse and began to smoke. When the cockpit got so hot that I felt fire was imminent, I made up my mind to set the ship down ... [Descending] to two or three hundred feet, I lowered my flaps and fired all my guns. This slowed me [and] I landed safely.

Martin called in his position and after spending the night in the bush he was rescued the next day by the Delissaville Aboriginal settlement superintendent, Jack Murray, and four Aboriginal trackers. Andrew's feet were so badly gashed as he struggled across the coral he had to be carried by stretcher. He was hospitalised before being returned to the US.

While the 7th and 8th Pursuit Squadrons had lost four pilots, the experience of 9th PS was more

Snooker tables lie amongst debris in the damaged recreation room at RAAF Darwin, hit during the raid on 27 April 1942.

satisfactory. Two flights under First Lieutenants Joseph Kruzel and James Porter had been scrambled, with Second Lieutenant Mitchell Zawisza claiming a Betty shot down. A further flight was ordered off, but no enemy aircraft were encountered.

While the *Argus* newspaper of 29 April reported the destruction of seven Japanese aircraft, the American pilots claimed three Bettys and four Zeros with two Zeros as probables. The Japanese lost one bomber flown by FPO2c Katsumasa Ozaki while ten aircraft were damaged. The scout plane was also lost near Koepang, with FPO1c Tadashi Kobayashi going down with the C5M machine. The Zero pilots claimed 13 aircraft shot down and six probables, while the Betty gunners claimed one aircraft shot down.

The 27 April raid was the last for the month and the Japanese held off, albeit unintentionally, during May, allowing the 49th PG a period of stabilisation while maintaining patrols and having flights on alert for possible raids. There was one raid launched on 15 May, with nine Betty bombers, but the mission was aborted in the face of bad weather.

Two days later, on 29 April, tragedy struck at Batchelor when two P-40s were scrambled. One flown by Lieutenant Jack Dale veered across the path of a second aircraft flown by Second Lieutenant Jack W Tyler causing him to lose control.

Dale's aircraft slammed into the Lockheed C-40 transport aircraft of Brigadier General Harold H George, which had just arrived at the base. The collision killed Second Lieutenant Robert D Jasper, and badly injured George, as well as a passenger journalist Mel Jacoby. Both George and Jacoby were transferred to the 119th Australian General Hospital at Adelaide River, however both were beyond help and they died.

Their bodies were recovered from the hospital, and George's was treated with much ceremony due to the reverence in which he was held, as an Australian newspaper later reported:

> Only, a week ago, on April 22, Brigadier-General George was awarded the Silver Star for gallantry in action during the campaign in the Philippines. A squad of Air Corps troops waited at an Australian aerodrome yesterday as a guard of honour for the bodies which were being flown from the scene of the accident.

One of the most brilliant air commanders in the United States Army, Brigadier-General George came to Australia with General MacArthur after commanding the air forces in the Philippines. During the World War, Brigadier-General George became an ace and won the D.S.O. He was an authority on pursuit aviation. He was 49 years of age.

George was buried with full military honours in Melbourne, while Jacoby was cremated, and his ashes scattered over Melbourne's Port Phillip Bay. Jasper was buried at the Batchelor War Cemetery and was later repatriated to Hawaii.

Meanwhile, the Battle of the Coral Sea was fought in early May, well out to sea from Queensland. This made a major check on Japanese ambition, with a combined American and Australian force fighting a carrier action where all of the combat was by aircraft; the vessels of each side never sighted each other. The Japanese came out ahead in terms of ships sunk or damaged, but their plan to invade Port Moresby, the capital of Papua and a key Allied air base, was thwarted. Despite that, the Battle of the Coral Sea became the precursor to much hard and bitter land and air fighting in New Guinea that would last for the next three years.

By May 1942, the 49th PG, under Lieutenant Colonel Wurtsmith, had a listed strength as follows:

Unit	Officers	Enlisted Men
Hq and Hq Squadron	20	270
7th Pursuit Squadron	37	194
8th Pursuit Squadron	33	163
9th Pursuit Squadron	34	334
49th Interceptor Control Squadron	3	367
445th Ordnance Co. (Aviation) 3rd Platoon	1	40
445th Ordnance Co. (Aviation) 1st Platoon	1	39
Replacements		59
	129	1,316

The 43rd Air Materiel Squadron, while operating closely with the 49th PG in maintaining its aircraft and providing replacements, was assigned to the 46th Air Base Group at Adelaide River and was not included in the overall 49th PG organisational structure.

Both the 27-Mile and 34-Mile airstrips had developed steadily during March. Elements of the 9th PS had moved into 34-Mile from 30 March under the orders of Major General Edmond Herring:

> ... to start moving P-40s there immediately ... and the 9th team was proud to have the first "all American" airstrip in operation.

Informally 34-Mile was known as Livingstone in memory of their first fatality in combat, Second Lieutenant John D Livingstone. The name Livingstone Field was officially recognised on 14 May.

A pilot poses with the sign to Livingstone Field. The 27- and 34-Mile airstrips built on the main north-south road were named Strauss and Livingstone in honour of deceased 49th PG pilots lost in April 1942.

Camouflage netting covers a 49th PG P-40 at RAAF Darwin. Such camouflage was integrated with the natural jungle cover and was very effective, as no P-40s were lost to air attack during the 1942 campaign. (Pacificwrecks)

It was not until early May that the 8th PS began moving to 27-Mile. On 11 May, they:

> ... installed themselves in the new camp at the newly completed 27-Mile strip southeast of Darwin. With the exception of a small camp at Connelly [Camp Connelly, in Darwin's suburban Winnellie] to maintain operations at the Fighter Sector, the 8th Sq was now the most advanced base of the 49th ...

As the US personnel occupied the new airstrips, squadron personnel adapted to the new conditions. The unsealed runway and taxiways caused problems with engines, instruments and particularly the 0.50-inch calibre machine guns, which required constant cleaning and lubrication. Meanwhile the 7th PS was operating from Batchelor, so all three squadrons were now well to the south of Darwin in bases they would occupy for the remainder of the campaign.

The USAAC airmen were likely most impressed though by the end of the wet season, which is usually very precise in its termination at the end of April. The Top End humidity drops sharply; the rains end, and temperatures even descend below 20° centigrade at night. During the days, although maximum heat levels are high, clouds disappear, and the flying weather is perfect.

On 28 May the 49th Pursuit Group became the 49th Fighter Group while its three squadrons were redesignated Fighter Squadrons. Other units within the Group, including the Interceptor Control Squadron, became the Fighter Control Squadron, *vide* General Order 15 of 4 June 1942, in response to a War Department Radiogram, No. 1918 of 27 May. The 43rd Air Materiel Squadron also became the 43rd Service Squadron. In another major administrative change at this time, the United States Army Air Corps had been redesignated as the United States Army Air Force (USAAF).

A fuselage section of a Betty bomber on display at the Darwin Aviation Museum. Several Bettys were downed by P-40s over Darwin in April 1942. (Author)

Betty bombers are waved off from Koepang on their way to bomb Darwin, in a colour sketch made for Japanese propaganda purposes. (Bob Alford)

CHAPTER 7

The Peak: June 1942

In having avoided Darwin during May, the Takao *Ku* recovered its losses while elements of No. 3 *Ku* were held ready to support the Port Moresby invasion operations which resulted in the Battle of the Coral Sea. While the outcome of the battle received little attention in the Darwin area, to the Japanese Prime Minister, Hideki Tojo, it provided an ideal propaganda opportunity:

> As a greater part of the fleet protecting Australia disappeared in the Coral Sea battle, Australia will have to reconsider her attitude towards Japan - otherwise she will have to suffer the consequences.

Australia's Prime Minister, John Curtin, responded:

> In Australia we play test matches to a finish - Tojo started this game.

Meanwhile the 49th FG and the Fighter Control Squadron (FCS) continued to develop the system for intercepting the enemy raids. Radar had improved though its range was only 80 miles, while cloth grid maps or "target maps" of the local area were issued to pilots. Each was gridded – numbered horizontally and lettered vertically – allowing quick referencing once the coordinates were given by the FCS. On the flatbeds of two adjoining trucks the FCS also developed a plotting room. Even then the system still relied heavily on the visual observations of Corporal Bill Woodnutt's group on Bathurst Island.

At the FCS headquarters a central "nerve centre" was set up and connected by teletype machine with telephone connections to the individual squadrons at their three different locations. By June the system was reported as:

> … meeting with some measure of success.

Replacement aircraft were also flown in from southern depots to make up for losses in combat and through accidents. Pilots were not so easy to replace, and June was marred by the deaths of four pilots. Only one of these deaths was caused by combat.

The first of three fatal accidents was on 5 June, when Second Lieutenant Ed Miller of the 8th FS dived into the ground from 10,000 feet. An 8th FS crew chief, Joe Cunningham, later wrote that:

> … at three PM, Lieutenant Miller was killed in a power dive. He didn't have his oxygen mask along with him …

There was another related casualty: Second Lieutenant William C Herbert, a close friend of Miller was taken off flying as a result of despondency and acute nervousness over Miller's death.

Three days later Second Lieutenant William H Payne dived into the ground in similar circumstances. It took some time to locate the aircraft. Fellow 7th FS pilot Second Lieutenant

Robert G Oestreicher wrote to Payne's family, and explained that the searchers:

> … finally did find it in the bush … what I could find of him the squadron doctor and myself buried in the crater with the plane … I said a few words … and the enlisted men fired some shots over him.

On 11 June Second Lieutenant Donald Dittler was forced to abandon his aircraft when the engine caught fire over Fountain Head south of Adelaide River. Landing safely in bush near Brocks Creek, Dittler was picked up and returned to Strauss.

Second Lieutenant Arthur "Doc" Fielder was not so lucky. Joe Cunningham wrote that he was on a training flight on 23 June when:

> … Lieutenant Fielder was killed when his engine failed him. Other pilots in the element … reported his plane stalled in a steep bank and fell out in a snap roll which developed into a spin at low altitude … [and he] crashed in a timbered area, the plane bursting into flames immediately.

The Japanese made up for lost time with sustained attacks on Darwin over four consecutive days from 13 June 1942. They lost only two Zeros of a total of 119 sent on the raids which supported 108 Bettys. It was a harsh turnaround for the Americans after the successes achieved by the 49th FG in April.

In the first raid on 13 June, 26 Betty bombers of an original 27 led by Lieutenant Commander Goro Katsumi attacked the RAAF base. The Bettys were accompanied by a very strong escort of 45 Zeros led by Lieutenant Takahide Aioi, a China veteran who had recently assumed command of No. 3 *Ku*. Plotted by radar, 36 P-40s were scrambled to intercept the force. In the ensuing combat three P-40s were lost to the Zeros.

Captain Robert D Van Auken of the Group's HQ & HQ Squadron was on a local flight with First Lieutenant Ben S Brown when he was directed to investigate an unidentified aircraft over Darwin. With Brown unable to keep up as he was flying a machine with a worn engine, Van Auken finally reached the bombers' altitude south of the Melville Island, one of the two immense islands lying north of Darwin. He made a stern attack, reporting:

> …the enemy were still on my tail. They shot at me and my plane caught fire.

After bailing out he was shot at in his parachute descent. Badly burned, he landed near Cape Gambier and was later located by three Aboriginal men.

Van Auken was fortunate. One of the men who found him was "Old Johnny" Barangbadla who, despite the barrier of the American accent, understood the pilot's injuries. Old Johnny ensured that Van Auken's scorched and painful legs were treated with a local vegetable paste remedy. Despite a pungent smell, the medication enabled Van Auken to sleep through the night.

The following day, Old Johnny and two others transported the weakened American pilot across to the mainland by canoe. On reaching Shoal Bay, one man remained with Van Auken while two others made their way by foot to the RAAF base. They led an RAAF ambulance back to the spot and Van Auken was taken to Kahlin Hospital. After some weeks of rehabilitation, he returned to the United States.

Van Auken's aircraft was later found buried in a mangrove swamp. John Gribble of the Snake Bay aboriginal settlement reported that one box of ammunition was the only item possible to recover. Gribble was an interesting man. By September 1942 he had formed a Snake Bay Patrol of 35 indigenous men who received military training and achieved a high level of discipline and military efficiency. Old Johnny was one of the men who served for over three years with the force, and who eventually received an ex-gratia payment of £200 for his services in the 1960s. Gribble was presumed for some years to have issued a second, ignored warning to Darwin about the incoming air armada of 19 February, but this has been disproved.[1]

Three 8th FS pilots, Second Lieutenant Lieutenants Charles C Johnson, Richard Dennis and Monroe Eisenberg, managed to land their combat-damaged aircraft. Second Lieutenant Harold Martin of the 7th FS force landed near the Daly River mouth. Rescued by nearby Australian troops he was returned to his unit. The aircraft was later salvaged by the 43rd Service Squadron.

The second P-40 lost was that of Second Lieutenant Pierre L Alford of the 8th FS. Bailing out after having been shot up by a Zero, two Zeros attempted to strafe him in his parachute. They were forced away by Second Lieutenant Earl R Kingsley also of the 8th FS, who spotted:

> … two small planes going north along Shoal Bay … Both planes attempted to strafe the parachute. I … could see tracers from both planes … I dived on them to prevent them strafing again.

Following the combat, the American pilots claimed one Zero downed, while the Japanese claimed ten P-40s and two probables. The *Kodochosho*, however, notes the Japanese lost two Zeros flown by FCPO Katsuji Matsushima and Flyer1c Mikio Tanikawa to an "unknown cause", while five Bettys were reported as having sustained damage and some crew casualties.

On the next day, 14 June, No. 3 *Ku* despatched 27 Zeros under Lieutenant Tadatsune Tokaji on a low-level strafing mission against Darwin. The force was detected at around 60 miles distance, bearing 325°at 1253 Darwin time. They were over the town 21 minutes later. Plotted by radar and reported by Bill Woodnutt's crew, they were intercepted by P-40s of the 7th and 9th Fighter Squadrons.

The Americans claimed four Zeros shot down. Second Lieutenants Andrew Reynolds, IB Jack Donalson, John D Landers (all of the 9th FS) and Captain Nathaniel H Blanton (of the 7th FS) each claimed a Zero.

The 9th FS flight leader, First Lieutenant Andrew J Reynolds, was leading Second Lieutenants Donalson, Landers, Ed Ball and Sid Woods, and reported:

> I was leading my flight of P-40s … when we first sighted the enemy … We were above them about 3,000 ft … I saw two Zeros going down in flames and one other out of control … I

---

1   See *Carrier Attack Darwin 1942*. "Appendix 8. Myth: The Gribble radio warning."

didn't get a chance to make any more passes at the enemy as there were too many Zeros ...

Despite Reynolds' observation, the Japanese reported no losses in the combat action.

The Zero pilots, equally over-confident of their kills, claimed five P-40s destroyed and three probables. The reality was just one loss, that of Second Lieutenant Keith D Brown of the 7th FS who was forced to abandon his burning aircraft over the 11-Mile transmitters of Naval Wireless Transmitting Station Coonawarra. Brown suffered a broken thigh and severe burns. Stan Goodwill, a naval rating at Coonawarra, recalled that:

> The poor devil was terribly burnt from the waist down. Our station ute rushed him to Darwin. Whether he survived I'll never know.

Nevertheless, the pilot was photographed, not looking too upset, on a stretcher shortly after his ordeal. The photograph was captioned:

> Brown can't say enough about the wonderful treatment received from the 2/12. He was also awarded the Purple Heart.

This was a medal awarded – as is the case still today – to US forces members wounded in battle. Brown did survive and spent two months in hospital before being evacuated to America.

On 15 June 27 Bettys led by Lieutenant Tanemasa Hirata appeared over Darwin with an escort of 21 Zeros led by Lieutenant Takeo Kurasawa. Approaching Darwin at 22,000 feet the bombers released 108 x 70-kilogram firebombs (incendiaries) and 216 x 60-kilogram bombs at 1145, targeting the wharf area, town, the naval Oil Fuel Installation and the naval victualling yards. Bombs detonated in a line from Kahlin Hospital at Larrakeyah through the town, the Police Paddock and to the wharf and harbour. The naval victualing yards, McMinn St powerhouse, the railway line, phone lines, residential houses and the *Army News* office were all damaged. Two AIF Privates, FW Finney and C Moore and two civilians, NR Moggs and LJ Giess, were killed in the bombing.

The Japanese aircraft were intercepted by 28 P-40s. The Japanese suffered no losses despite claims of six Zeros and a bomber damaged. The Zero pilots claimed six P-40s destroyed along with three probables; three "Brewster Buffaloes" and an unidentified aircraft were also claimed.

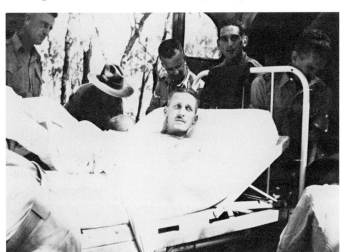

Second Lieutenant Keith D Brown is loaded into an ambulance after bailing out south of Darwin on 14 June 1942.

Damaged buildings in Smith Street following the 15 June 1942 raid on Darwin.

Second Lieutenant Claude S Burtnette of the 7th FS was forced to bail out over Quail Island after a 20mm round exploded in his starboard wing. Landing in the water he started swimming while Captain Bill Hennon flew cover. Two and a half hours later Burtnette reached shore. He was picked up that evening by the RAN patrol vessel *HMAS Kuru* and returned to Darwin.

Another victim of the Zeros, Second Lieutenant Clarence T Johnson, attacked a Betty but was in turn attacked by a Zero, damaging the canopy and engine of his P-40. After firing on another bomber, his engine caught fire and he bailed out over Bynoe Harbour, west of Darwin. Landing near a spring he set up a small camp and then wandered away, hoping to reach food caches which had been placed near the coast. However, Johnson became hopelessly lost, and after spending five days in dense mangroves he was found by Jack Murray and his trackers from Delissaville. It was sheer good fortune for Johnson that Murray and his trackers were in the area searching for another pilot, Second Lieutenant Harris (see below). Murray had stopped the engine on his launch at the insistence of tracker Willie. Johnson later reported:

> I learned they were a searching party looking for me ... they had searched for two days. They later told me they had no idea I was there and had not heard my calls until the motor was stopped.

Johnson was returned to Darwin via the lugger *HMAS Ibis,* commanded by Lieutenant Erik Sodersteen, RAN.

A further mission was flown by the No. 3 *Ku* on 15 June when two elements each of a Babs escorted by three Zeros flew reconnaissance sorties over Darwin during the late morning. No intercepts were made and the aircraft returned safely to Koepang.

The following day, 16 June, the Japanese mounted their fourth straight day of operations with 27 Bettys led by Lieutenant Tanemasa Hirata departing Koepang. The escort was by 27 Zeros under Lieutenant Takahide Aioi. Approaching the target area from the northwest and turning south for Darwin town over East Point, from 25,000 feet the Bettys released 20,520 kilograms of bombs at 1128. The bombs "walked" through town, injuring 11 persons, severely damaging the Bank of New South Wales in what is now the Smith Street Mall, and Jolly's Store. They also hit oil tank Numbers 10 and 11 at the Oil Fuel Installation and set them ablaze, and damaged the railway yards and the AWA coastal radio station that used the callsign "VID".

Casualties were light, however. One Australian soldier, Private TJ Griswood, a member of the

Lieutenant Chester T Namola

Lieutenant Chester T Namola was from Trumbull County, Ohio. He was decorated with the Purple Heart after his death. He is memorialised at the Tablets of the Missing, Manila American Cemetery, Manila, in the Philippines.

Lieutenant Chester Namola a few days prior to his death on 16 June 1942. (USAF)

7th Military District ambulance train unit, died of injuries the following day.

Eighteen P-40s of the 8th and 9th Fighter Squadrons intercepted the force in a combat action that took them west over Cox Peninsula as the Japanese exited from the Darwin area. A frustrated Second Lieutenant James L Porter reported the bombers were:

> … first sighted … at about 28,000 ft and to our left. We were flying at 25,000 ft which was our ceiling … The enemy was so high above us we could not make an attack.

Indeed, the Japanese suffered no losses. Three 8th FS P-40s were lost however, and a pilot, Second Lieutenant Chester T Namola, was posted missing in combat and has yet to be located. Namola simply disappeared. Flying as wingman to First Lieutenant Randall Keator, he was last seen as the four-plane flight attacked the bombers southwest of the Tiwi Islands. Keator reported:

> We started in to attack and before reaching the bomber formation three Zeros dropped their belly tanks … we could not get to the bombers, so we dived away from them, and that is when I lost my wingman.

Second Lieutenant James H Martin landed in the shallows off Cape Gambier when his engine overheated following combat. Repeating his 27 April landing at Gilruth Point, he swam ashore. Tying himself to a tree for the night he used his parachute to ward off mosquitos and midges. He was rescued the following day by a naval vessel replenishing coastal food dumps.

Meanwhile, the 8th Fighter Squadron's Second Lieutenant William B Harris was in trouble. Part of Captain George Kiser's flight, Harris was attacked by three Zeros before diving away and then climbing to attack the bombers on their exit from Darwin. During his attack his guns stopped firing and he dropped away and headed for base. Harris reported:

> On sighting land I had only ten gallons of gas left … so I decided to land … The landing gear collapsed shortly after the plane hit the ground and … burst into flames almost immediately. I sat by the airplane until 5:30 … and then decided to attempt to reach a food cache.

Harris was stranded in inhospitable country near Hatters Hill to the southeast of Fog Bay. It was a further three days before he was spotted by a No. 12 Squadron Wirraway and later picked up in a Tiger Moth flown by Flight Lieutenant Walter D Pye of the RAAF's No. 34 Squadron.

Three other P-40s force landed as a result of combat damage. Lieutenant Andrew Reynolds of the 9th FS landed near Berry Springs after his coolant radiators were damaged in combat. Second Lieutenant John Fisher failed to lower his undercarriage at Batchelor. Second Lieutenant Robert McComsey of the 9th FS force landed his badly damaged aircraft at the 147th Field Artillery range north of Adelaide River.

During the four-day period from 13-16 June the 49th FG losses were heavy, with the Bettys claiming three P-40s downed for two Bettys damaged, while the Zeros claimed eight P-40s shot down and six probables. In return the 49th FG claimed 13 enemy aircraft destroyed. However, the ledger was clearly in favour of the Japanese. Eight P-40s were downed during these combats, in return for the loss of two Zeros and no Bettys. This largely vindicated a change in the Japanese tactics since their heavy losses in April. In June they approached the target zone from a higher altitude and with a much stronger fighter escort.

After having flown four missions in four days, the Japanese crews enjoyed a brief respite with no further Darwin missions for the rest of June.

Meanwhile, one USAAF man from Darwin was doing sterling service in Melbourne. Reported under the headline "Impressions of US Officer" in *The Age* newspaper, Colonel LaRue was addressing members of the "Carry On Club" about his memories of February:

> The things he remembered most vividly, said Colonel LaRue, were the magnificent coolness and devotion to duty of the Australian anti-aircraft batteries, the weakness of our defences against the Japanese attackers, the way in which slit trenches proved of immense value in protecting and saving the lives of those who used them, the gallantry of Allied pilots who went aloft to engage the raiders, although hopelessly outnumbered; and the perfect formation and methodical bombing methods of the Japanese aircraft ...

> As to his general impressions of Australia, Colonel LaRue said, like most American officers and men at present in this country, he was deeply touched by the friendly and cordial attitude of the Australian people towards the US forces. He appreciated and acknowledged also the spirit of co-operation in evidence amongst the officers and men of the Australian fighting forces towards their American allies. The bonds of understanding and friendship which had been established between Australia and America in the past six months would not be easily broken.

A P-40 with its engine removed for servicing at Strauss, showing the outdoor maintenance which was the norm during the 1942 dry season. (Bob Alford)

Four P-40s of the 9ᵗʰ Fighter Squadron's B Flight in a tight formation with Captain Joe Kruzel's #80 Bicky closest to the camera. (Bob Alford)

CHAPTER 8

Final Months: July – September 1942

By the end of June both the No. 3 *Ku* and the Takao *Ku* were at full strength after having made good their losses earlier in the month. Even allowing for scheduled maintenance and repairs at Kendari and Koepang, the units still posed a formidable threat. Indeed, the lull in raids after the mid-June "Blitz" was both a relief and a concern to the Allies. To the 49th Fighter Group in particular, after gaining the upper hand it seemed that the Japanese had either failed to press home their advantage or were otherwise employed.

It was a bit of both, as the RAAF Official History explains:

> During June intelligence reports suggested that the Japanese intended to occupy Tual, on the south of the main island in the Tanimbar Group, and Dobo in the Aru Group. Apart from their proximity to Darwin these bases, and particularly Dobo, were contiguous to Dutch New Guinea where some furtive Japanese activity was reported.

At Batchelor and the roadside airstrips maintenance was carried out during the lull while replacement aircraft were ferried to the squadrons. Not all of these ferry flights were formally planned, as Clyde Barnett recalled:

> … in late June or early July … [we] got leave for 7 days in Melbourne … most of the transports were coming and going from Batchelor … We took off fairly early … got to Adelaide and arranged to spend the night there. The next day we flew to Melbourne … When our time was expiring we started to think about transportation and ran into CC Johnson … he made arrangements for us to ferry 4 P-40s back to Darwin. What a nice deal.

On 10 July the lull was over when two reconnaissance aircraft were reported over the Darwin area. Some 36 fighters were scrambled but no contact was made. A second radar plot was later identified by Second Lieutenant Stewart W Robb of the 8th FS as being that of RAAF Hudsons.

Two days later the 9th FS lost two pilots in a mid-air collision. Four aircraft led by Second Lieutenant IB Jack Donalson along with First Lieutenant Dick Taylor, Second Lieutenants George E Preddy and John S Sauber were on a training flight. They were over Manton Dam when Sauber made a mock attack and collided with Preddy's aircraft, crashing and rolling into a rocky gully in flames. Donalson later recalled:

> I was flying Sauber's wing when the accident happened … Dick and I circled, until Preddy landed … [then I] got help and went to the crash site and recovered Preddy and … Sauber. Sauber's body was still in what was left of the cockpit … Sauber was too close when he started his pass … before he could break off … he collided with Preddy.

Preddy bailed out and parachuted to safety, badly injuring his leg as he landed. After recovering in a

Inside the USAAF Officer's Club at Strauss, 1942. (Bob Alford)

Melbourne hospital, he was assigned to the European theatre where he became a leading American ace. He was shot down and killed by American anti-aircraft fire on Christmas Day, 1944.

Three days later, on 15 July, a reconnaissance of the Darwin area was flown by a Babs escorted by four Zeros, all from the No. 3 *Ku*. The aircraft departed Koepang at 0900 and were over Darwin at 1250. However, radar had seen them coming, with the aircraft plotted at 332 degrees and 74 miles out at 1157 Darwin time.

Twenty P-40s were scrambled to intercept. Three Zeros were reported directly over Fannie Bay at 1202 Darwin time before they flew away. However, no interception was made, and the Japanese aircraft landed safely back at Koepang at 1430.

With the Takao *Ku* tied up with supporting the operations in the Tanimbar and Aru Islands, the Japanese commenced harassing night raids by one or two *shotai* of Bettys over Darwin. The first came on 25 July following a directive to attack outlying islands in the Arafura Sea, while Darwin was to be attacked from that date.

The attacks commenced with a raid on the RAAF base, civil aerodrome and military installations by two *shotai* of Bettys led by Lieutenant Tanemasa Hirata on the night of 25 July. The AA searchlights were unable to illuminate the aircraft and the AA batteries did not engage as a result. Unhindered, the Bettys released their bombs and returned to Timor. The bombs released by one *shotai* landed in The Narrows area between the RAAF base and the civil aerodrome, hitting the water pipeline and dislocating power and telephone lines. The bombs released by the other *shotai* were scattered harmlessly over Bynoe Harbour.

The following night, 26 July, two *shotai* of Takao *Ku* Bettys each dropped 27 x 60-kilogram bombs and 9 x 70-kilogram incendiaries. The targets were the RAAF base, the old Vesteys meatworks at Bullocky Point and the Darwin town area.

Led by Lieutenant Makino, the two flights departed Koepang at 1800 and 1915 and subsequently approached Darwin at 22,000 feet. They released their bombs at 2135 and 2223. The searchlights were waiting for them and made sightings, and the AA batteries engaged the raiders. However, no hits were made, and the bombers exited Darwin to the northwest. In this attack three houses were destroyed, two others were badly damaged and some fuel was lost.

At 1900 on 27 July three Bettys armed with 36 x 60-kilogram bombs approached Darwin at 24,000 feet. The aircraft released their bombs at 2200. The ordnance landed at 10-Mile, at Knuckeys Lagoon where a searchlight was damaged and at the RAAF station where pyrotechnics were ignited and an unserviceable Wirraway was damaged. The searchlights were unable to locate the raiders and as a result the AA batteries did not engage.

The Japanese bombers were over Darwin again on the night of 28-29 July to attack the RAAF base. Three Takao *Ku* Bettys armed with 36 x 60-kilogram bombs took off from Koepang at 2155 and approached Darwin at 22,000 feet. They released their bombs at 0052 on 29 July. The searchlights and AA batteries tracked and briefly engaged the raiders. Damage was reported to the runway and the water pipeline.

Some hours later, a further raid followed that same night of 29 July. Six Takao *Ku* Bettys armed with a total of 48 x 60-kilogram bombs and 24 x 70-kilogram incendiaries took off from Koepang after midnight. Approaching Darwin as individual *shotai* at 24,000 feet the Bettys released their bombs at 0355 and 0440 respectively. A first stick fell in the area of the Oil Fuel Installation, the Oval AA site (now the Cenotaph) and Mindil Beach, while a second stick severely damaged the searchlight workshops at Knuckeys Lagoon and dislocated power lines. The bombs of the second *shotai* fell harmlessly into the bush.

Both flights then flew over the Darwin area for some time, more for nuisance and psychological value perhaps, until 0445 and 0450 before turning for home, where they landed at 0715 and 0730.

In the early hours of 30 July three Takao *Ku* Bettys armed with 27 x 60-kilogram bombs and 9 x 70-kilogram incendiaries took off from Koepang at 0103. They had planned an attack on the Darwin town area and the RAAF base. Approaching the target zone at 24,000 feet, although illuminated by searchlights, the aircraft released their bombs at 0348. Severe damage was reported to the RAAF Mechanical Transport Section, while a truck was destroyed and power lines dislocated. The AA batteries engaged ineffectively.

The night raid of 30 July was followed the next day by the first daylight raid in six weeks, when 26 Bettys with an escort of 27 Zeros attacked the RAAF base. Radar detection was made at 1209 Darwin time and at 160 miles distance. Thirty-six P-40s were scrambled, allowing them the opportunity to gain height for an interception. Two flights from the 7th FS attacked the bombers as they approached Darwin, reportedly forcing two Bettys to drop from the formation in flames.

Flying on and approaching the RAAF Station from Lee Point, the Bettys released their bombs at 1305 (Tokyo time) resulting in the death of Flying Officer RDJ Tregonning at the RAAF Station, damage to a Hudson bomber, and the destruction of fuel (112 drums of condensed fuel and 26 drums of 90 octane fuel). The main runway was cratered and the water mains cut.

The Japanese lost a bomber and one Zero, with four Bettys damaged during the combat. The P-40 fighters claimed six Zeros and three Bettys with three of each as probables.

The defenders lost one aircraft but no lives. Second Lieutenant Gene F Drake of the 7th FS was forced to bail out after being "bounced" by two Zeros as he struggled with an overheating engine and loss of oil. Drake landed on a beach west of Darwin, as recorded by Ralph Boyce in his diary:

> … [he] landed safely in the water near a beach and was last seen … doing handsprings … Later, Melikian and Fisher flew up to see that he was OK and saw him, stark naked, taking a sun bath in the crash boat.

With the 23rd *Koku Sentai* occupied further east in the Aru and Tanimbar Islands, and with an expected lull in raids, the 49th Fighter Group took the time to bring the aircraft up to strength, though accidents continued to keep the squadron mechanics and the 43rd Service Squadron busy.

However, as was the norm in WWII, accidents and technical failures took their toll. On 2 August Captain Mitchell "Eck" Sims was forced to crash land at the 43rd Service Squadron base at Adelaide River when he found his engine was failing to throttle back. Extending full flaps, he landed at high speed and ground looped the aircraft to avoid trees. Two days later Second Lieutenant Fred Hollier, the 9th Fighter Squadron's Operations Officer, was taxiing from one revetment to another when he ran into some trees, damaging the propeller and a wing. A week later Second Lieutenant John Landers misjudged the length of the Livingstone airstrip and hit a log as the aircraft lifted off. Proceeding to Adelaide River he landed wheels up and handed the aircraft over to the 43rd Service Squadron.

Yet more accidents followed. On 16 August Captain Joe Kruzel force-landed after his engine cut out at high altitude and two days later First Lieutenant George Manning was on an air-to-air gunnery flight when he flew into the target cable, shearing it and damaging a wing. The whipping cable then tangled itself in the tailwheel of Captain Jim Selman's P-40. Both landed safely.

While the mechanics and repair shops were being kept busy, Colonel Wurtsmith was attached to General Douglas MacArthur's Headquarters in Brisbane from 7 August. Wurtsmith was busy not only in meeting the demands of MacArthur's Headquarters, but in planning for the impending move of the 49th FG to New Guinea.

At the squadrons, training flights were commenced to improve tactics and air-to-air gunnery, the latter providing, as First Lieutenant Jesse Peaslee wrote:

> … the first opportunity for many pilots to do scored shooting. Much time was [also] spent in squadron formation, simulated attacks on bombers and ground positions, and dive bombing … the accuracy was good with very little practice.

Bombing practice was also carried out over Indian Island using 500-pound bombs, some of

A 49th FG P-40 demonstrates a fast take-off from Strauss Field. After an accident-prone beginning, during the course of 1942 the group became very efficient at quick take-offs. (Michael Claringbould)

them damaged following a recent fire at the Batchelor bomb dumps. Even with these training flights each squadron maintained at least one flight on alert during daylight hours, while patrols were also maintained.

With personnel all awaiting news of an expected move from Darwin, a sign that the 49th FG might be on the move was the arrival of ground personnel of No. 77 Squadron, RAAF, at Batchelor on 12 and 14 July. Like the Americans, the RAAF squadron was also equipped with P-40Es.

The move of the RAAF unit had been preceded by a 25 July visit to the 49th Fighter Group by the commanding officer of No. 77 Squadron, Squadron Leader Dick Cresswell. He met with Air Commodore Bladin and Wurtsmith, amongst others, to make arrangements for the impending move north by his unit.

The ground element of No. 77 Squadron commenced its long overland journey from Pearce in Western Australia on 1 August, while 21 P-40s departed over two weeks later on 17 August. Two were involved in accidents at Alice Springs and were left behind while the remaining 19 aircraft arrived at Batchelor on 18 August. The first Australian fighter squadron in the area, as recorded by Jesse Peaslee:

> … meant a great deal to everyone. It was the first step towards the Australian forces taking over the whole area, and foretold a movement of part or all of the group.

Operating from Batchelor the RAAF squadron commenced operational training almost immediately, however the program was interrupted on 23 August when the Japanese reappeared over the Darwin area.

Twenty-seven Bettys escorted by 27 Zeros mounted an attack on Hughes Airfield. This was in answer to a Directive made at the Grand Imperial Headquarters in response to Allied operations in the Solomons:

> … as soon as the Allied forces took offensive action … in the Solomons area in early August 1942, the war situation suddenly became concentrated in that area … to check the enemy operations in the Solomons area, our Navy air force … carried out a day attack on PORT DARWIN … on 23 August, and night attacks on 24 and 25 August.

The force approached the Australian coast over Fog Bay. They had sighted the Perron Islands when twenty four 49th FG P-40s attacked well out to sea after receiving ample warning by radar

For Victory
Examiner

101st YEAR OF PUBLICATION

I, TASMANIA, TUESDAY, AUGUST 25, 1942

Registered at the General Post Office, Hobart,
for transmission by post as a newspaper.

PRICE 2d.

WHAT THE FARMER WANTS TO KNOW
News for the Poultrykeeper.
Have You a Legal Problem?
CONSULT THE POPULAR WEEKLY,
"THE WEEKLY TIMES"
AND GET THE ANSWERS.
NOW ON SALE

GRAD

HEADACHE FOR HITLER

DARWIN FIGHTERS BAG
13 JAP. PLANES

Interceptors Smash Raiding Force

By George H. Johnston, "The Examiner" War Correspondent

SOMEWHERE IN AUSTRALIA, Monday.—"Our best day's duck hunting yet," was how an official spokesman at General MacArthur's Headquarters to-day described the brilliant performance of Allied fighter pilots in completely smashing up a heavy Japanese raid on Darwin yesterday.

More than a quarter of the entire Japanese attacking force of 47 planes was destroyed, four Japanese heavy bombers and nine Zero fighters being shot down in combat without loss to our defending fighter force.

It was the best record of any air operations in the S.W. Pacific area since the war began. The enemy attacked Darwin about noon with 27 heavy bombers, flying at an extreme altitude of 25,000 feet, escorted by a screen of 20 Zero type fighters. Our

fensive reconnaissance bombed enemy buildings and the wharf area with unobserved results.

Pilots' Stories

From Axel Olsen

Somewhere in Australia, Monday.— Pilots said after the Darwin raid that some dogfights were at very close range. A lieutenant said: "I don't know how far away from one Zero I was, but I could see the pilot's face under a red cap. I don't know what sort of cap it was but his face looked

Aircraft to Beat Subs.

SAN FRANCISCO, Monday.— Henry J. Kaiser, West Coast shipbuilder, announced to-day that he has teamed with Mr. Howard Hughes, millionaire airplane designer and movie producer, to build 500 cargo planes, in the most ambitious aviation programme the world has ever known to beat the submarine menace.

ALL MUST BE GIVEN UP FOR VICTORY

"In this war, the full significance of which we have not yet entirely realised in Australia, there is no profit, no individual advantage, no piece of individ-

The front page of the Launceston Examiner on 25 August 1942 which included the headline "Interceptors Smash Raiding Force". After the disastrous 19 February raid, positive stories from the Darwin front were very important to Australian morale.

and directions from No. 5 Fighter Sector. One Betty was downed northwest of Point Blaze with the loss of its eight crew, while two others were damaged and returned to Timor. One of these had an engine shot out and crash landed near Dili.

The remainder of the formation bombed Hughes accurately, destroying a Wirraway, a Brewster Buffalo, 250 drums of fuel and 240,000 rounds of 0.303-inch ammunition. The runway was damaged but there were no reported casualties.

In the air, the Japanese lost four Zeros and their pilots. One crashed near Emu Springs, likely the victim of Second Lieutenant Charles C Johnson of the 8th FS who reported downing a Zero over Fog Bay:

> … just before the enemy reached the coast … [I] shot a Zero down in flames.

After bombing Hughes, the Bettys continued east before turning north over Cape Hotham and then west over Cape Jarlheel en route to Timor, all the while harried by the P-40s.

The P-40 pilots claimed eight Zeros destroyed plus three probables while six Bettys were also claimed as downed. In turn the Japanese pilots reported combat with six P-40s, five "P-39s" and two unidentified fighters, claiming 11 destroyed and two probables. One 7th FS pilot, Second Lieutenant Fred O'Riley, was jumped by Zeros over Cape Hotham and force-landed his damaged P-40 on the shores of Finke Bay east of Darwin. His aircraft was salvaged by a 43rd Service Squadron crew the following day.

From an Allied standpoint, the interception and reported enemy losses were a striking success that had not been repeated since the Anzac Day raid of 25 April. The headline of the *Argus* newspaper of 25 August read:

Japs Lose 13 Planes in Darwin Raid. Brilliant Allied Interception.

General MacArthur was quick to send his congratulations to the new Allied Air Forces commander, Major General George Kenney:

For General Kenney Stop My Heartiest Felicitations to intercepting units of Darwin yesterday Stop That is the way to do it End.

A more relevant message from Colonel Wurtsmith on 25 August read:

Quote Set up the beer on me damn good work quote Wurtsmith Unquote.

The newspapers were even more ecstatic. The Launceston *Examiner*, for example, reported that:

Our tactical interception, which was carried out by American-piloted Kittyhawks, was one of the most brilliant ever seen. The Kittyhawks ripped through the Japanese formations, cutting down four heavy bombers from the enemy bomber formation and sending down in flames nine Zeros which gave combat.

All our planes came through the fierce aerial clash without loss, and the enemy bombers, probably driven off their target to some extent by the ferocity of our interception, dropped their bombs wildly in the aerodrome area with negligible results.

The fighters of Darwin are rapidly building up a magnificent record against the Japanese ...The Darwin formations are brilliantly trained under an American colonel; their morale is high, and the pilots include some of the best-known pursuit pilots of the Philippines and Java fighting.

Effective Technique

It is apparent that with Kittyhawks they have evolved a fighter technique that is brilliantly effective against the reputedly deadly Zero.

The Zero shot down over Fog Bay was later located in September 1942, when a RAAF Unexploded Ordnance (UXO) team assessed the site. Some items were later recovered and forwarded on to Allied Intelligence by Lieutenant Erik Sodersteen RAN, commander of *HMAS Ibis*, who put the UXO team ashore.

Following the 23 August raid, Zeros weren't seen over the Darwin area for the remainder of 1942. In the meantime, the Japanese reverted to flying night bombing "nuisance" attacks as directed by the Grand Imperial Headquarters.

The "Screamin' Demons" insignia of the 7th FS. By the time of its move to New Guinea, many of the 49th FG P-40s had acquired colourful artwork. (Michael Claringbould)

A raid by six Betty bombers was carried out on 24 August. The formation was illuminated by the searchlights and engaged by anti-aircraft fire around 2100 as it attacked the RAAF base. Bombs fell in a line from the civil aerodrome to Parap Camp, badly damaging army buildings, straddling the railway and dislocating power and telephone lines. Another raid was carried out on the night of 26-27 August, with bombs falling in a line from the Botanic Gardens to Parap Camp, while severely damaging the AWA Coastal Radio Station "VID".

While no serious damage was reported in such bombing raids, the attacks were a source of frustration throughout the Darwin area. Ralph Boyce wrote in his diary:

> Beautiful tropical moon, soft gentle breezes – bah! Between the Nips and the mosquitoes we had a hell of a night last night. There must be something about moonlight that attracts insects and pests.

At Strauss sleep was also disrupted. Joe Cunningham complained:

> The darn Japs came over today at 4:00 AM and woke me out of a sound sleep … They dropped a lot of bombs.

Another raid by two *shotai* of Bettys took place on the night of 30-31 August. The first *shotai* dropped 36 x 60-kilogram bombs over Darwin and caused slight damage to an oil pipeline. Searchlights were unable to pick up the intruders. The second *shotai* dropped its bombs ineffectually over the Cox Peninsula.

Notably the 49th FG was not trained in night operations, and their fighters were kept on the ground during the series of July-August night raids amid a general feeling of frustration. In response a determined pilot, First Lieutenant James Morehead of the 8th FS, decided to attempt to intercept the raiders in the early hours of 31 August. This was after his CO, Captain "Eck" Sims, refused his request to take-off. However, after becoming airborne Morehead quickly became disoriented. This was not surprising: Darwin was blacked out, and he would have been able to see very little except for the searchlights. Presumably he hoped they would have lit up the bombers for him, and he may well have been able to see their exhausts glowing red in the distance.

With his plan unsuccessful Morehead was able to land at Hughes, his first night landing in a P-40. He later recalled:

> Last but not least … came the chewing out by the Sq. and Group commanders. Oh, for the life of a fighter pilot!

Airmen inspect the crater caused by the bomb which near-missed the P-40 Star Dust at Livingstone in the early hours of 26 September. (Bob Alford)

Morehead was subsequently grounded, for both the unauthorised flight and for having forced the Hughes airfield lights to be illuminated in blackout conditions to let him land.

In a precursor to the impending move of the 49th FG, the Headquarters and Headquarters Squadron was officially disbanded in a formal parade on 31 August, during which Lieutenant-Colonel Hutchinson announced that the Group had been cited for its actions in the Darwin area. Congratulatory messages were read from General MacArthur, Major General Kenney and by the commanding officer Wurtsmith.

After arriving at Batchelor on 18 August, No. 77 Squadron was non-operational for the remainder of the month, mainly flying training and area familiarisation flights. By this time the wet season was due to begin and a general lull in Japanese operations until early 1943 was expected. Hence as the 49th FG began its move to New Guinea, in September No. 77 Squadron assumed responsibility for the air defence of the Darwin area (it would be joined by a second RAAF unit, No. 76 Squadron).

However, before the 49th FG fully departed the Northern Territory it had one final brush with the Japanese. This occurred in the early hours of 26 September when three Takao *Ku* Bettys dropped bombs on Livingstone Field. The 9th FS diarist recorded:

> Several bombers made two or three trips over our camp area, finally dropping a load of bombs across the northern end of the runway. One hit less then fifteen feet from an airplane, but did no damage. There was also one small hole in the runway, but there was no other damage or casualties.

The near-missed P-40 was named *Star Dust* and belonged to Lieutenant Andrew Reynolds. Ironically, this was the closest that Japanese bombers got to damaging the 49th FG on the ground during the whole campaign. The camouflage and dispersal pens built at Darwin, Batchelor, Livingstone and Strauss had worked very successfully.

An element of four 49th FG P-40s in formation over typical northern Australian terrain in 1942. While training in New South Wales in February, Colonel Wurtsmith had emphasised the importance of formation flying to his pilots. He got the nickname "Squeeze" following his repeated exhortations to wingmen to "squeeze in closer".

CHAPTER 9

Postscript

After leaving Darwin, the 49th Fighter Group saw much fighting in New Guinea and later the Philippines. During 1943 it exchanged its worn P-40Es for P-40K/Ns, before re-equipping with twin-engine P-38 Lightnings. The 49th FG would become the highest scoring USAAF fighter group with 667 aerial victories by the end of the war. This was a remarkable record for a unit which commenced operations in Australia with so many untrained and inexperienced pilots in early 1942. Much of this record is due to the efforts of Colonel Wurtsmith and his leadership group, who laid the foundations for this success during the 1942 Darwin air campaign.

Following the massive 19 February raid by carrier-based aircraft on Darwin, the Japanese enjoyed a brief period when they assumed air superiority over the northern Australian town in the absence of Allied fighter opposition. The arrival of the 49th FG as an efficient and functional interceptor force was something of a surprise, with a good deal of success achieved in April when Betty formations came in at moderate altitudes and with a modest escort of Zeros.

Conditions became more challenging from June onwards when the Bettys kept to high altitudes, sometimes over the effective ceiling of the P-40s, and with greatly reinforced escorts. Nevertheless, what the 49th FG achieved was laudable, especially given that the P-40 had never been designed as an interceptor and performed poorly at high altitude.

The record of the 49th FG in 1942 is also very impressive when compared to the record of No. 1 Fighter Wing, RAAF, which defended Darwin during the 1943 dry season. No. 1 Fighter Wing was equipped with the Spitfire Mk VC interceptor which gave its best performance at high altitude, and the wing arrived in the Darwin area fully confident of sweeping the Japanese from the skies. However, amid technical setbacks and failed "Big Wing" tactics, the experience of No. 1 Fighter Wing was decidedly mixed and also served as a reminder of the exceptional quality of the Japanese pilots which the 49th FG had faced.

Perhaps the most remarkable aspect of the 1942 air campaign was that despite fighting against the deadly Zero flown by highly experienced No. 3 *Ku* pilots, the 49th FG lost just four men killed in combat. This says much about the structural integrity of the Curtiss-built fighters, and also the advantage of fighting over friendly albeit inhospitable terrain. Many downed American pilots had the indigenous population to thank for their survival, perhaps none more so than Captain Robert Van Auken. After being badly burned and bailing out over the Tiwi Islands, Van Auken was rescued by "Old Johnny" Barangbadla who delivered him safely to a Darwin hospital after a long ocean-going canoe journey.

Although only four pilots were killed in combat (Livingstone, Strauss, Fish and Namola), death through accidents was common and some 30 members of the USAAC / USAAF that were killed in the Northern Territory in 1942 are listed in Appendix 2. The sacrifice of these men must never be forgotten by Australians.

While Australians and Americans fought together in the First World War, it can be argued that the real origins of the enduring Australian-American alliance stem from the events in Darwin in early 1942. In particular, it was the 19 February attack on Darwin that largely shocked Australia out of wartime complacency and drove home the true vulnerability of Australia itself. That experience was shared by many Americans present, including those fighting desperately on the destroyer USS *Peary* and in the skies above.

In the grim days that followed 19 February 1942 it was the young Americans of the 49th Pursuit Group who came forward to defend Australian soil. Their successes were subsequently broadcast to a grateful nation and did much to improve morale.

Ironically in recent times the accents and swagger of American servicemen has made a welcome return to the streets of Darwin, as a regular deployment of the United States Marine Corps is based in the town.

Seen in New Guinea in April 1944 after landing his Lightning on a newly constructed airstrip is Brigadier General Paul Wurtsmith (second from left), who was in charge of 5th Fighter Command. After commanding the 49th FG in 1942, Wurtsmith was promoted and became one of the stand-out senior officers of the Fifth Air Force. On the far right is Colonel Bob Morrisey, Wurtsmith's chief of staff who had commanded the 7th PS in early 1942. On the far left is Air Commodore Frederick Scherger, RAAF, who was the area commander in Darwin when it was raided in February 1942. (Australian War Memorial)

Appendix 1 – The Oestreicher Incident

It might seem strange to place what was once thought to be a sterling story of action at the back of a book as an appendix. But the tale deserves such a place – it was a fabricated story that has no place alongside the heroism of the USAAC pilots fighting on 19 February 1942 over Darwin.

Of ten American fighters defending against the Japanese air raid of 19 February 1942, only the P-40 of Lieutenant Robert Oestreicher survived. Uninjured, he landed his machine, allegedly heavily damaged, almost two hours later. He said he downed two dive-bombers.

The truth is different. Oestreicher was a novice fighter pilot with just 14 hours on P-40s before leaving the USA. When he saw Japanese aircraft he dived away to save himself and hid in clouds. His aerial claims were invented. In 1982 he returned to Darwin where he lied further about his fight. He has become, in books, magazines, museum exhibits and articles, a hero of the biggest aerial attack on Australia. But none of it is true.

The record needs to be set straight: it overshadows the true heroism and sacrifice of the other nine fighter pilots who flew in Darwin's defence that day.

Oestreicher's Account

At 1145, by his later reports, Oestreicher landed at the RAAF base, now a smoking ruin. His aircraft was undamaged except for a burst tyre. His commanding officer and three of his fellow pilots were dead.

The story of Oestreicher shooting down two aircraft appeared in no official USAAF accounts, and is not in the Lowe Report, the comprehensive examination of the raid carried out shortly afterwards. It was on 21 July, four months later, that Oestreicher composed a report:

> After flying among the clouds for about half an hour I spotted two Series 97 dive bombers with fixed landing gear on a course heading for Batchelor Field. Intercepting them at about fifteen hundred feet I fired and saw one definitely burst into flame and go down. The other was smoking slightly as he headed for the clouds. I lost him in the clouds.

> Later that same afternoon a report came through that a coast artillery battery had located both planes within a mile of each other. These were the first confirmed aerial victories on Australian soil.

This is complete invention. No such dive-bombers were shot down – none have been found and neither are such losses mentioned in the Japanese records. No reports from a "coast artillery battery" – and there were several situated on both East and West Points defending Darwin Harbour – have been located.

If any US pilot had shot down two Japanese aircraft it would have been cited; indeed lauded, and the pilot's name celebrated by his own force. The raid was extremely widely reported in hundreds of newspapers – there is nothing in any newspapers or official reporting of the time. The Lowe report said "one Japanese dive-bomber and one Zero fighter" had been brought down in the action: the wrecks of both these had been found.

Oestreicher's statement makes little sense and is littered with contradictions. He claimed he saw two dive-bombers "on a course heading for Batchelor Field". Why would any aircraft fly south? The aircraft carriers were to the north, and even a novice pilot – and these were veterans of Pearl Harbor – could navigate visually with the distinctive land features of Darwin harbour and the two Tiwi Islands to the north, in perfect flying weather of blue skies and scattered clouds. Why would any bomber pilot leave the protective cover of the Zero fighters? The Vals only carried one 250-kilogram bomb, and once it was delivered, left the vicinity immediately. Every second over the target area was dangerous, with thousands of troops firing rifles at the attacking aircraft, in addition to the heavier fire of many anti-aircraft weapons.

Oestreicher says this was "half an hour" after the initial contact. This is ridiculous: the Vals carried one bomb, and if a pilot was lost, he would have ditched the bomb, and headed north. The raid lasted likely only 20 minutes at a maximum, with the Kates bombing first and leaving, and the Vals expending their bomb and also departing. What Oestreicher was actually doing for the next hour after the raid had ended is unknown. What he should have been doing was refuelling and re-arming, hopefully to be in a position to attack any future raid.

Oestreicher was indeed witness to the second Darwin raid that struck around 1145. He then claimed to have met with Brigadier General Patrick Hurley:

> I went to the Twelve Squadron Hangar and there reported to Captain Wheelas [sic] and General Patrick Hurley what had happened and that I thought I had shot down one plane and that the other might be classed as a "probable". The following morning I took off at dawn and flew to Daly Waters where a Squadron Leader Connely took charge of repairing my plane. Later that same afternoon a report came through that a coast artillery battery had located both planes within a mile of each other.

None of this was recorded by Hurley's aide Lieutenant Bobb Glenn, in his later account of this period. If Oestreicher had shot down two aircraft it would have made him the hero of the hour, but there is no such description. Glenn's party took shelter from the second raid and obtained a car to take the general south immediately.

The next morning, by his own account, Oestreicher flew his P-40 to Daly Waters airstrip, 400 miles to the south, where he remained for several days, carrying out flights he later dubiously labelled Combat Missions. On 27 February he received orders to join a new unit in NSW. But the next day he heavily damaged his P-40 during a landing accident in Queensland. He continued to Amberley, onboard a Dutch Lodestar that had been accompanying him.

At this time Oestreicher met one of the other pilots, McMahon, in hospital in Brisbane. McMahon recalled that Oestreicher was using the unusual circumstances for his own advantage. Possibly this was the only time the only pilot who had escaped unscathed from the 19 February raid met any of the surviving pilots from the action. Oestreicher (along with all of the other P-40 pilots) was soon awarded the Distinguished Service Cross by General MacArthur. Notably he was not given a higher decoration, which would have been the norm if he had shot down two of the enemy.

How did the "two bombers downed" story arise?

As there was no squadron structure to confirm and record the air-kill claims, as would normally be the case, how did they arise? Two official American histories, of 1944 and 1948, do not mention Oestreicher's claims. The first of these, *The Army Air Forces in World War II*, describes the Darwin fight, with the names of pilots, and concludes:

> Only Lt Robert G Oestreicher managed to bring in his bullet-punctured P-40 to a normal landing.

The second, *The AAF in Australia to the Summer of 1942*, has less detail, and says simply:

> Aircraft losses for the Allies totaled 9 P-40s shot down.

Oestreicher had been telling his two bomber story from 1943. A letter to his father said:

> I have two Nip notches on my belt … My ship was pretty well shot up having some sixty odd holes in it … The two ships were confirmed by a coastal artillery unit.

An American paper, the *Miami Student*, reported:

> … he had finished off one Jap bomber and crippled another. He landed with 60 bullet holes in his plane.

Other papers reported similarly, and Oestreicher was widely feted.

The two-bomber story first arises in book form in 1951 in Walter Edmonds' *They Fought with What They Had*. This covers US air operations in the Western Pacific from December 1941 until March 1942. Edmonds drew on interviews from 169 airmen of the Pacific War. As so few official records exist regarding this period, this book is well regarded, and perhaps has the status of a quasi-official history. Edmonds tells us:

> Only Oestreicher fought his way clear and then, finding himself alone among the Japs, flew south into the clouds, from which a little while later he ambushed two dive bombers, shooting one down … Oestreicher came in at 1145 to refuel and rearm his plane and change a damaged wheel.

Edmonds wished to portray brave and heroic Americans battling against insurmountable odds; he admits much material was received verbally and relied on recollections, which, he said:

> … may not make for definitive history in the eyes of military scholars.

The 19 February accounting is thinly sourced, with none of the P-40 pilots interviewed.

In 1957 the Official History of the Royal Australian Navy was published. On the subject of the air battle over Darwin, without sources, it reports Oestreicher as shooting down one fighter, and two dive-bombers. The Australian Army History, published two years later, reported:

> Oestreicher got into cloud cover, from which he later shot down two bombers, and brought his bullet-marked machine home.

Then in 1962, the RAAF Official History cited Edmonds as their source, but strangely credited Oestreicher with a Zero fighter rather than a Val dive-bomber.

Popular books appeared telling the story, but it took three decades for Oestreicher to receive an official USA credit. In 1978 the *USAF Credits for the Destruction of Enemy Aircraft, World War II* cites Second Lieutenant Robert G Oestreicher, 33 Pursuit Squadron (Provisional), for a single air victory on 19 February 1942.

In 2010 William Bartsch's *Every Day a Nightmare* noted that in several cases Oestreicher's story was contradictory, and in particular his account "does not jibe with those of two surviving pilots" – Wiecks and McMahon. This was followed in 2011 by Bob Alford's authoritative *Darwin's Air War*, and in 2013 by Tom Lewis and Peter Ingman's *Carrier Attack Darwin 1942*. Both works, having access to Japanese records, suggested the claim was impossible. Alford, Lewis and Ingman stated definitively the losses of 19 February:

Type	Carrier	Crew	Fate
A6M2 Zero BII-124; #5349	*Hiryu*	Flyer3c Hajime Toyoshima	Crash-landed Melville Island; pilot captured and made POW.
A6M2 Zero	*Kaga*	Flyer1c Yoshio Egawa	Wing damaged after hitting a tree; ditched near carriers; pilot rescued
D3A1 Val AII-254; #3304	*Kaga*	Flyer1c Takezo Uchikado FCPO Katsuyoshi Tsuru	Shot down by ground fire near RAAF Darwin. crew KIA; buried at the site; later disinterred and buried at the local Japanese war cemetery; later disinterred and reburied at the Cowra War Cemetery, New South Wales, Australia.
D3A1 Val	*Soryu*	Flyer1c Takeshi Yamada Flyer1c Kinji Funazaki	Ditched near carriers; crew rescued.

The rest of Oestreicher's flying service was undistinguished. Indeed, it appears he had many problems flying in combat conditions and was eventually transferred. In 1982 the pilot returned to Darwin for the 40th anniversary of the raid. There he was interviewed by media and historians. His account of the downing of the Vals includes:

> Got them both and we verified it the next day when some of the RAAF ack ack boys **and myself** [author emphasis] went out there. They took a piston off one of the engines and cut it in half and made the ashtray that I have brought back now and gave to the Lord Mayor because I believe it belongs in Darwin.

The piston ashtray has survived and is held in the Lord Mayor's office in Darwin. But it could have been made from one of the many thousands of the type of engine it came from. It is notable Oestreicher's story had changed by his 1980s visit to have him visiting the crash site;

previously he had just said his "two kills" had been confirmed by others. The "RAAF ack ack boys" also does not ring true: the Army operated the anti-aircraft sites. Notably, there are no accounts of any visit to Oestreicher's supposed wreck in any of the several accounts of the 19 February raid written by AA gunners, nor in their unit war diaries.

The presentation of the piston smacks of plotting, and an attempt to take advantage of the stories of heroism Oestreicher knew were false. His visit to Darwin was surrounded by well-wishers, presentations, and journalists' interviews. He was presented with a plaque by the residents of Cox Peninsula. The social gatherings must have been quite lively, and he would have been the hero of the hour.

Oestreicher, in a fashion characteristic of witnesses not telling the truth, gets his facts consistently wrong. This is why suspects in police investigations are interviewed several times, and they are asked to tell their story again, often to their indignant "I've told you this already" protest. The technique is to see if the person is looking into their memory and recounting what is indeed there, or whether they are telling something they have made up – and which is therefore much more difficult to remember. Oestreicher consistently gets the facts of the aircraft he "shot down" wrong: they are Kates; then dive-bombers, then single-seat dive-bombers, then a Kate/single seat fighter, and then a Zero. The truth is there were no such victims at all.

Robert Oestreicher died in Wichita, Kansas, on 10 January 1991 aged 73. He has achieved some fame for his supposed action. A poster of Oestreicher in action has since been created, and a postcard of the same print. Modern books continue to repeat the story. He is a featured character in the electronic Defence of Darwin Experience displays at the Darwin Military Museum.

But Oestreicher should not be commemorated for anything more than flying in the defence of Darwin. He was not a hero of the 19 February raid, and this should be established so it does not obscure the actions of those in the sky, on the ground, and in ships, who shot back at the Japanese air armada.

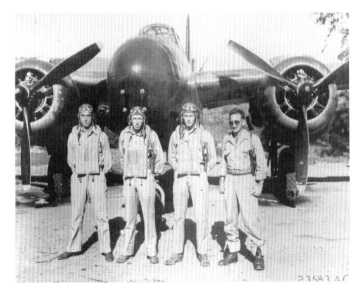

Oestreicher (right) in New Guinea where he briefly flew A-20s before returning to the US in 1943. (Alford Collection)

Appendix 2

Members of the USAAC / USAAF killed in the Northern Territory, 1942.

Date in 1942	Rank and Name	Aircraft	Details	Lives lost	Cumulative total – lives lost
15 Feb	Lieutenant Robert Buel	P-40	Attack on Mavis flying boat north of Tiwi Islands	1	1
19 Feb	Major Floyd Pell	P-40	Air combat with Zeros	1	2
19 Feb	Lieutenant Jack Peres	P-40	Air combat with Zeros	1	3
19 Feb	Lieutenant Elton Perry	P-40	Air combat with Zeros	1	4
19 Feb	Lieutenant Charles Hughes	P-40	Air combat with Zeros	1	5
19 Feb	Staff Sergeant Hugh M McTavish	Consolidated LB30 Liberator AL521	Killed on the ground when aircraft strafed by Japanese attackers	1	6
14 Mar	Second Lieutenant Frank L Stiertz	P-40	Landing accident	1	7
16 Mar	Lieutenant Albert H Spehr	P-40	Flying accident	1	8
19 Mar	Second Lieutenant John J Musial Second Lieutenant Neal T Takala	P-40 P-40	Navigation accident	2	10
4 Apr	Lieutenant John D Livingstone	P-40	Hit by friendly fire after combat with Zeros; died in crash landing	1	11
21 Apr	Corporal Anthony A Gattamelata Corporal Ray E Love Private First Class Wiley H Wiley Private William Bedord Private John J Faris Private Walter M Feret Private Robert W George Private Nick Hinich Private Richard D Schmidt Private Buford H Willard	Guinea Airways Lockheed Super 14 VH-ADY *Adelaide*	Killed in flying accident during travel flight, Annaburroo Station NT. Aircraft not located until 25 June 1942.	10	21
27 Apr	Captain Allison W Strauss	P-40	Lost in combat with Zeros	1	22
27 Apr	Lieutenant Owen R Fish	P-40	Lost in aerial combat	1	23
29 Apr	Brig General Harold H George Second Lieutenant Robert D Jasper	C-40	Killed in transport aircraft struck by P-40 in take-off accident at Batchelor	2	25
5 Jun	Lieutenant Ed Miller	P-40	Died in accident resulting from a power dive	1	26
8 Jun	Lieutenant William H Payne	P-40	Training accident	1	27
16 Jun	Lieutenant Chester T Namola	P-40	Missing after air-to-air combat	1	28
23 Jun	Lieutenant Arthur Fielder	P-40	Training accident	1	29
12 Jul	Lieutenant John S Sauber	P-40	Training accident – mid-air collision	1	30

Sources

Books

Alford, Bob. Darwin 1942. *The Japanese attack on Australia.* Osprey. 2017.

Alford, Bob. *Darwin's Air War.* 1942-1945. AHSNT. 2011.

Assistant Chief of Air Staff, Intelligence Historical Division USAAF. The AAF in Australia to the Summer of 1942. Army Air Forces Historical Studies: No. 9. July 1944.

Bartsch, William H. *Every Day a Nightmare. American Pursuit Pilots in the Defense of Java, 1941-1942.* Texas A&M University Press. 2010.

Cooper, Anthony. "The Territory Remembers Darwin 1942: the missing year." For The Territory Remembers. 2017.

Edmonds, Walter Dumaux. *They Fought with what They Had.* Boston; Little Brown & Co. 1951.

Ferguson, SW and Pascalis, William K. *Protect & Avenge. The 49ʰ Fighter Group in World War II.* Schiffer. 1996.

Gillison, Douglas. *Royal Australian Air Force 1939-42.* Canberra: Australian War Memorial. 1962.

Glover, Ralph C. Lt. Col. *The History of the 808ʰ Engineer Aviation Battalion 15 September 1941 to 12 January 1946.* Pages 58-60. Copy held RN Alford courtesy Professor Alan Powell CDU.

Griffith, Owen. *Darwin Drama.* Bloxhall and Chambers. 1946.

Hata, Ikuhiko and Izawa, Yasuho. (Translation by Gorham, Don C.) *Japanese Naval Aces and Fighter Units in World War II.* Airlife. 1989.

Hess, William H. *49ʰ Fighter Group. Aces of the Pacific.* London: Osprey Publishing. 1998.

Izawa, Yasuho. *From Rikko to Ginga.* Asahi Sonorama. 1995.

Johnson, Sue, and Winspear, Brian. (Eds.) *Tasmanians at War in the Air 1939-1945.* Brian Winspear: Hobart, 2002.

Lewis, Tom. *Darwin's Submarine I-124.* South Australia: Avonmore Books, 2011.

Lewis, Tom. *The Empire Strikes South.* South Australia: Avonmore Books, 2017.

Lewis, Tom and Peter Ingman. *Carrier Attack.* South Australia: Avonmore Books, 2013.

McDowell, Ernest K. *49ʰ Fighter Group.* Squadron/Signal Publications. 1989.

Morehead, James B. In My Sights. *The Memoirs of a P-40 Ace.* Self-published. 2003.

Mulholland, Jack. *Darwin Bombed.* Bookbound Publishing, NSW, 2009.

Noah, Joe and Sox, Samuel L. Jr. *George Preddy Top Mustang Ace.* Motorbooks International. 1991.

Sakai, Saburo. *Samurai.* New York: Ballantine Books, 1957.

Tagaya, Osamu. *Mitsubishi Type 1 Rikko 'Bettty' units of World War 2.* Osprey. 2001.

Unpublished sources

Alford, Bob: various personal files

Barnett, Clyde W. Diary extracts 1942. War Memories 1941-1945. Self-Published. 1995.

Boyce, Ralph J. Personal diary 1942. Transcribed to Vols 1-III by Alford 1988.

Cunningham, Joe. Extracts from diary relating to the 8th Squadron. 1942.

McEwin, Gavin. Commentary on Darwin's Air War. 1992.

Woodnutt, Bill. Correspondence to Bob Alford. 2 January 1992.

Reports and official documents and histories

Australian War Memorial file, AWM 54 Item 423/4/92.

Boniece, Robert J and Scott, Louis T. Historical Record 49th Fighter Group USAAF. AAF Historical Office. 18 November 1946.

Brett, George H. Lt Gen. Report. U.S.A. Air Corps Units in Australia. Appendix 4. Station List. 6 May 1942.

Historical Division, Assistant Chief of Air Staff, Intelligence. The AAF in Australia to the Summer of 1942. Army Air Forces Historical Studies No. 9. July 1944. Hurst, R. J. R. Lt Col. Fortress Commander.

JACAR (Japan Center for Asian Historical Records). Kodochosho for Takao Ku, 28 March 1942.

National Institute for Defence Studies. Office of the Chief of Military History. Department of the Army. Japanese Monograph No. 92. Southwest Area Naval Operations Apr. 1942 – Apr. 1944.

National Institute for Defence Studies. *Senshi Sosho.* Chapter Nine of Military history Department, National Institute of Defense Studies, the Defense Agency. *The Dutch East Indies and Bengal Bay Area: Naval Advance Operations].* Vol. 26. Tokyo: Asagumo Shinbunsha, 1969. Translated by Haruki Yoshida & Dr Peter Williams.

National Institute for Defence Studies. Kawano, Teruaki. Kawano, Captain Teruaki. The Japanese Navy's air-raid against Australia during the World War Two. August 29, 1997.

Maxwell AFHRA. USA. 9th Squadron Journal.

Office of Air Force History Headquarters USAF. Albert F. Simpson Historical Research Centre Air University. USAF Historical Study No.85. USAF Credits for the Destruction of Enemy Aircraft, World War II. 1978.

NAA File: AWM52 4/16/5 2 Heavy Anti-Aircraft Battery (2 Hvy AA Bty) 1941 – 1944 1149353.

NAA File: AWM52 4/16/18 14 Heavy Anti-Aircraft Battery (14 Hvy AA Bty) 1940 – 1945 1150559.

National Institute for Defense Studies of the Ministry of Defense (Japan). Dai 3 koukutai hikoukitai hensei koudouchyousyo shyouwa17nen 3gatsu 4nichi.

Peaslee, Jesse. Activities of the Ninth Pursuit Squadron. 1943.

Sanford, Clarence E. Combat Report. Lieutenant Sandford's (sic) Experiences at Horn Island. Report of 22 November 1942.

USAAF. Forty Ninth Fighter Control Squadron (SEP.) Army Air Forces. Squadron History. Book II. Page 1. Courtesy Lt Col. Horace 'Ho' Levy. (Bob Alford Collection)

USAAF. Adams, Brig Gen. Message NR252 to USAFIA, dated 4 February 1942. (Bob Alford Collection)

USAAF. Fitch, B. M. Lt Col. Secret Message 452.1/3 Operational Control of the 49th Pursuit Group. 11 February 1942. (Bob Alford Collection)

USAAF. 'Secret' message Brett to Adjutant General ACS-3, ACS 620. Dated 5 March 1942. (Bob Alford Collection)

USAAF. Message Wurtsmith to HQUSAFIA 49-BNR-41-A 19/3 of 19 March 1942.

Interviews

Haslett, Gary. *P-40 Over Darwin*. Interview with Lieutenant Robert McMahon. "Kittyhawk Down." DVD. 2013.

Roberts, Lysle. Spitfire pilot. 90 second vignette. *The Territory Remembers*. Northern Territory Government, 2016.

Harada, Kaname, Zero pilot. Nagano, Japan, June 2015, with questions written by Dr Tom Lewis, presented in Japanese by Hiromi Loveday.

Newspapers & Magazines

Various articles held by Tom Lewis & Bob Alford

Index of Names

Aioi, Lieutenant Takahide   70, 80, 83

Alford, Second Lieutenant Pierre L   49, 81

Andrew, Second Lieutenant Stephen   73

Ashazawa, FCPO Noboru   67

Asihiro, Lieutenant Taketoshi   65

Bader, Douglas   35

Ball, Second Lieutenant Ed   81

Barangbadla, "Old Johnny"   80, 81, 97

Barnett, Second Lieutenant Clyde H   43-45, 47, 49, 69, 71, 72, 87

Bedord, Private William   104

Bladin, Air Commodore Frank "Pop"   65, 91

Blanton, First Lieutenant Nathaniel H   50, 81

Boyce, Private Ralph L   44, 45, 48, 53, 90, 94

Brett, Lieutenant-General George H   49

Brown, First Lieutenant Ben S   80

Brown, Second Lieutenant Keith D   49, 82

Buckingham, Ron   41

Buel, Lieutenant Robert J   9, 13-15, 17, 104

Burnett, Air Chief Marshal Sir Charles   66

Burtnette, Second Lieutenant Claude S   83

Cameron, Captain Gordon   53

Channon, Pilot Officer   46

Chennault, Claire   60

Connely, Squadron Leader   100

Cory, Second Lieutenant Howard D   42

Coss, Captain Walter L   50

Cox, Flight Lieutenant BM46

Cresswell, Squadron Leader Dick   91

Cunningham, Joe   50, 52, 79, 80, 94

Curtin, Prime Minister John   79

Dale, First Lieutenant Jack D   50, 74

Davasher, Major Glen   2

Davis, Second Lieutenant George "Pinky"   45

Dennis, Second Lieutenant Richard E   50, 71, 81

Dittler, Second Lieutenant Donald   80

Dockstader, Second Lieutenant Robert B   50

Doherty, Captain John E   41

Donalson, Second Lieutenant IB Jack   81, 87

Drake, Second Lieutenant Gene F   90

Duke, Second Lieutenant Ben   49

Egan, Major John F   42

Egawa, Flyer1c Yoshio   102

Eisenberg, Second Lieutenant Monroe D   50, 69, 81

Eisenhower, Major-General Dwight D   43

Faris, Private John J   104

Feret, Private Walter M   104

Fielder, Second Lieutenant Arthur "Doc"   48, 49, 80, 104

Findlay, Fred   55

Finney, FW   82

Fish, Second Lieutenant Owen W   72, 73, 97, 104

Fisher, Second Lieutenant John   85, 90

Fujiwara, Lieutenant Takeharu   71

Fujiwara, Lieutenant Takeji   65-68

Funazaki, Flyer1c Kinji   102

Furakawao, FCPO Kinichi   14

Gardner, Second Lieutenant Grover J   67, 68

Gattamelata, Corporal Anthony A   104

George, Brigadier General Harold H   74, 75, 104

George, Private Robert W   104

Giess, LJ   82

Gilbert, Flying Officer Arthur   46

Glenn, Lieutenant Bobb   100

Glover, Lieutenant John   21, 23, 27

Glover, Lieutenant Colonel Ralph C   55

Goodwill, Stan   82

Gould, Nat   60

Gray, First Officer William T   53

Gribble, John   81

Griffith, Wing Commander   17, 18

Griswood, Private TJ   83

Hall, Noel   55

Harada, Kaname   32

Harris, Bomber   34

Harris, Second Lieutenant William B   83, 84

Hartmann, Erich   35

Harvey, Second Lieutenant Clyde L   54, 55, 65

Hector   55

Hennon, Second Lieutenant William J   50, 70, 83

Herbert, Second Lieutenant William C   49, 79

Herring, Major General Edmond   75

Hinich, Private Nick   104

Hirata, Lieutenant Tanemasa   72, 82, 83, 88

Hiroyoshi, Nishizawa   33

Hogan, John   48

Hollier, Second Lieutenant Frederick F   53, 90

House, Second Lieutenant AT   51

Hughes, Lieutenant Charles   21, 25, 27, 104

Hurley, GeneralPatrick   18, 100

Hutchinson, Major Donald   43, 95

Inada, Flyer1c Denichi   67

Iwasaki, Lieutenant Nobohiro   51

Jacoby, Mel   74, 75

Jasper, Second Lieutenant Robert D   74, 75, 104

Johnsen, Second Lieutenant Lester J   50

Johnson, Second Lieutenant Charles C   73, 81, 87, 92

Johnson, Second Lieutenant Clarence T   83

Kajalwal, Dodger   55

Kates, Corporal   47

Katsumi, Lieutenant Commander Goro   70, 80

Kawai, Lieutenant Shiro   51

Kawazoe, Lieutenant Toshitada   66

Keator, First Lieutenant Randall   84

Kelting, John A   68

Kenney, Major General George   93, 95

King, Second Lieutenant Joseph H   48

Kingsley, Second Lieutenant Earl R   73, 81

Kiser, First Lieutenant George E   50, 84

Kobayashi, FPO1c Tadashi   74

Kofukuda, Lieutenant Commander   60

Krupinski, Walter   35

Kruzel, First Lieutenant Joseph J   50, 74, 86, 90

Kurosawa, Lieutenant Takeo   54, 66, 72, 82

Kusuhata, Lieutenant Yoshinobu   66, 67

Landers, Second Lieutenant John D   68, 81, 90

LaRue, Colonel   85

Lee, Second Lieutenant Don   51

Livingstone, Second Lieutenant John D   48, 67, 68, 75, 76, 97, 104

Loft, Pilot Officer   46

Love, Corporal Ray E   104

MacArthur, General Douglas   11, 24, 25, 75, 90, 93, 95, 101

Maeda, Yoshimitsu   33

Makino, Lieutenant   89

Manning, First Lieutenant George   90

Marika, Wandjuk   52

Marlin, Sergeant "Pop"   49

Marshall, General George C   43

Martin, Second Lieutenant Harold   81

Martin, Second Lieutenant James H   73, 84

Masell, Patrick   60

Matsuda, Flyer1c Shigeoshi   67

Matsushima, FCPO Katsuji   81

McComsey, Second Lieutenant Robert M   53, 66, 85

McMahon, Lieutenant Robert   22, 27, 100

McTavish, Staff Sergeant Hugh M   22, 104

Melikian   90

Miller, Second Lieutenant Ed   79, 104

Moggs, NR   82

Molyneux, Lieutenant Cyril   68

Moore, C   82

Morehead, Second Lieutenant James B   50, 94, 95

Mori, FPO1c Shigiki   54

Morrissey, First Lieutenant Bob   47, 51, 52, 98

Murakami, FPO1c Shiro70

Murray, Jack   73, 83

Musial, Second Lieutenant John J   48, 104

Nagasawa, FPO1c Shinobu   54

Namola, Second Lieutenant Chester T   48, 84, 97, 104

Norton, Flying Officer JW   46

O'Brien, Major Gilbert   35

O'Riley, Second Lieutenant Frederick   47, 48, 93

Oestreicher, Lieutenant Robert G   13, 17, 19, 20, 22, 27, 80, 99-104

Oishi, FPO1c Genkichi   51

Overud, Second Lieutenant Carlyle   42

Ozaki, FPO2c Katsumasa   74

Payne, Second Lieutenant William H   79, 80, 104

Peaslee, Second Lieutenant Jesse   65, 90, 91

Pell, Major Floyd J   9, 13-15, 17-19, 21, 25, 27, 104

Peres, Lieutenant Jack R   21, 24, 27, 104

Perry, Lieutenant Elton S   21, 25, 27, 104

Poleschuk Second Lieutenant Stephen   54, 55

Porter, Captain GE   70

Porter, Second Lieutenant James L   66, 74, 84

Preddy, Second Lieutenant George E   58, 87

Pye, Flight Lieutenant Walter D   84

Ramsay, Captain Rosser B   43

Redington, Lieutenant William A   52

Redmond, Second Lieutenant Juanita   25

Regan, Dan   42

Reynolds, Second Lieutenant Andrew J   2, 50, 66, 68, 81, 82, 85, 95

Rice, Lieutenant Burt   21, 27

Rickenbacker, Eddie   35

Robb, Second Lieutenant Stewart W   87

Roberts, Lysle   33

Roosevelt, President   42

Roth, John   49

Rozum, Captain TJ   70

Sakai, Saburo   33, 34

Sanford, Second Lieutenant Clarence   52

Sauber, Second Lieutenant John S   68, 87, 104

Scherger, Group Captain   17, 18, 98

Schmidt, Private Richard D   104

Scott, John   55

Sells, Second Lieutenant William D   65, 66

Selman, Captain James   41, 47, 68, 90

Sims, Second Lieutenant Mitchell "Eck"   69, 90, 94

Sodersteen, Lieutenant Erik   83, 93

Spehr, Second Lieutenant Albert H   41, 104

Stagg, Ross   33

Stiertz, Second Lieutenant Frank L   48, 104

Strauss, Captain Allison W   50, 72, 73, 76, 97, 104

Takala, Second Lieutenant Neal T "Sonny"   48, 104

Takenaka, Rear Admiral Ryuzo   70

Tanikawa, Flyer1c Mikio   81

Taylor, First Lieutenant Dick   87

Tokaji   55

Tokaji, Lieutenant Tadatsune   55, 81

Tojo, Hideki   79

Toyoshima, Flyer3c Hajime   33, 102

Tregonning, Flying Officer RDJ   90

Tsuru, FCPO Katsuyoshi   102

Tucker, Flying Officer AD   46

Tyler, Second Lieutenant Jack W   74

Uchikado, Flyer1c Takezo   102

Van Auken, First Lieutenant Robert D   42, 43, 45-47, 49, 80, 81, 97

Vaught, Second Lieutenant Robert H   65

Walker, Lieutenant William   20-23, 27

Wass, Kevin   55

Wavell, General Sir Archibald   45

Wellstead, Bill   55

Wiecks, Lieutenant Max   20, 27

Wiley, Private First Class Wiley H   104

Wilford, Sergeant Norm   48

Willard, Private Buford H   104

Williams, Air Vice Marshal Richard   18

Willie   83

Wilson, Air Commodore   18

Winspear, Brian   19, 31

Woodnutt, Corporal Bill   65, 79, 81

Woods, Daphne   48

Woods, Second Lieutenant Sid   81

Wortley, Flying Officer R   S35

Wurtsmith, Major Paul B   40, 43, 45, 46, 50, 51, 65, 75, 90, 91, 95-98

Yamada, Flyer1c Takeshi   102

Yamagata, Lieutenant Shigeo   51

Yamaguchi, Lieutenant Sada-o   68

Zawisza, Second Lieutenant Mitchell   65, 74